PENCAK SILAT PERTEMPURAN

PENCAK SILAT
Stepping from stone to stone
PERTEMPURAN

Sean Stark

Stark Publishing

St.Cloud, FL

Published 2007
Printed by Lulu.com in the United States of America
Cover Design and book layout by Sean Stark

ISBN 978-0-6151-3968-5

Combat Silat
901 Delaware Ave.
Saint Cloud, FL 34769

combat-silat.net ° combat-silat.com ° combatsilat.us ° silat.us °
info@combat-silat.net

3rd **Edition** – First published in 2005 Stark Publishing.
Original work copyright © 2005.

DISCLAIMER: The author and publisher of this material is NOT RESPONSIBLE in any manner whatsoever for any injury which may occur through reading or following the instructions in this manual. The activities, physical or otherwise, described in this material may be too strenuous or dangerous for some people, and the reader(s) should consult a physician before engaging in them.

Acknowledgments

A special thanks to all those who have helped in any small way to make this book possible, this includes all those who have helped in the production of the accompanying electronic media pieces and those who have expressed interest in silat, additionally, a special thanks to all guru-guru silat who selflessly promote the beauty of pencak silat. Also, special thanks to my wife and children who have knowingly and unknowingly sacrificed time that this project would be completed. Lastly, thank you to my God for allowing me to complete this.

Pencak Silat Pertempuran
(Combat Silat)

Introduction and study guide

Preface

This book (it is hoped) will introduce you to the art known as Pencak Silat Pertempuran or more commonly known as Combat Silat. In addition, though this book was designed with the intent to introduce you to Combat Silat and our training methodology, it will also introduce you to the greater art of Pencak Silat generally. Due to the enormity of the subject, we can only begin the introduction and perhaps take a cursory glance at a few of the more advanced elements of Pencak Silat Pertempuran. Additionally, all of the errors in this book are strictly my own.

Hormat

Some of you who know me closely, know that my first priority in life is to my God. It is hoped, this book will bring Him Glory, Honor and Praise. May I be a living sacrifice to Him.

My second priority in life is to my beautiful family: Amy, Alyssa, Ashlyn and Ellie for without their support I would not be able to practice martial arts, let alone write this book.

Lastly, my hormat goes out to those teachers who have shared with me their passion for martial arts and their expression of it in its various forms. A special acknowledgement should be given to:

- Si Fu Ronald O. Skipper
- Si Fu / Guro Danial Molash
- Guru Bruno Cruicchi
- Guru Bayu Wicaksono
- Guru Hassan Ali Al-Ansari
- Guru Mushtaq Ali Shaw
- Guru Roedy Wiranatakasumah
- MaHa Guru Victor de Thouars

These fine teachers have contributed much to my understanding of martial arts generally and specifically. They have devoted themselves selflessly to the study and training in their respective arts and have passed on much knowledge to many. The knowledge you have given to me is of great value and I hope that I am able to bring honor to it through its dissemination, propagation and practice. Please forgive any mistakes I have made.

My Prayer: "Lord use me to communicate the true value of the arts these teachers have given to me. I ask that the wisdom and insight you have shared with me would be clearly presented in this manual and bring you the full glory, honor and praise you deserve. Amen!"

Chapter 1: Pencak Silat Pertempuran
Section 1: Introduction

First, a little about Pencak Silat Pertempuran, this system came into existence through a process of revelation (which was probably largely due as a result of head trauma). That is, this system of living and self-defense is a product of sudden revelations. It was not one large one but rather, many small ones. They continue today. The revelations came and continue to come in many forms, sometimes via the result of actions and sometimes they just "pop" into my head. The revelations were not always about fighting (although it is my belief that there is much to learn from the art of fighting that pertains to life) but many times the revelations were about human nature and about God. Sometimes learning about God has led to revelations about fighting, human nature and about God. That said there is no formula for understanding other than consistent desire and willingness to receive revelation.

Often revelation comes in forms that require us to change what we currently believe to be the truth. It is through this process of shedding that Truth begins to reveal itself.

The revelations I am talking about are not the same as being totally and completely enlightened as you may know about from religion, but rather it is a process of revelations and enlightening moments that continue to work even after the initial feeling of enlightenment has passed to teach and guide. This type of illumination is found through study, meditation, prayer and experience. Sometimes illumination from God appears spontaneous and miraculous but it is never that way. It is always the product of your intentional searching and desire to have the eyes of your heart opened and it is always carried out according to the Greater Plan of God.

It is my belief that nothing other than God illuminates. No amount of introspection or reflection without the guiding hand of God can illuminate one to understanding. No amount of reading others illuminated work can illuminate, it is only through the hands and eyes of God that Truth is illuminated or revealed. Now, let me state, that this does not mean that a person cannot gain insight by another persons actions, writings, statements, etc., rather, I mean to say that God prepares us to receive the illumination from those actions, writings, statements, etc. but God alone is the Great and Eternal Light. (See John 1:9)

Section 2: System Structure

There are many Pencak Silat styles in existence. Each has its own distinguishing characteristics, mannerisms and principles. You could say that each system has its own "flavor". Combat Silat is no different. Combat Silat is a campuran silat system based on several different systems of silat primarily. However, it is important that you know that

Combat Silat is NOT an eclectic art that borrows "cool techniques" from here or there. It is a single art, with a singular approach from A-Z. It is codified, direct and scientific in its approach to personal combat. The heart of Combat Silat comes from Pencak Silat Pamur and the wisdom contained in elements of its structure. It is not a concepts approach to martial arts, nor is it a mixed martial arts approach!

Pencak Silat Pertempuran's primary combat "flavor" is the understanding of the relationship between the adversary and the pesilat and the realization that without that relationship there is no combat. As such, Combat Silat utilizes a series of Ales (evasions) and Masukan (entries) that allow you to have a reference point for techniques, based on your position in relationship to the adversary's. Essentially, Combat Silat is a "GPS" system for personal combat.

Additionally, the structure of Combat Silat is unique as well. It is a simple modular approach, which means that one piece directly leads to the next piece of the system. Once the core system is understood, modules may be mixed and matched according to necessity. It can be a very adaptable and very dynamic system. The only real limitation is the individual practitioner of Combat Silat.

To continue, when taught, the basic positions are numbered one through eight. This applies to all core material. The numbering system is such that all number one methods work together (in the core system), all number two methods, all number three methods and so on throughout the system (the exception are those elements beyond the core 1-8). To illustrate, Ales Satu and Masukan Tangan Satu work effectively together, as does, Ales Satu, Masukan Tangan Satu and Masukan Kaki Satu. As does Ales Satu and Tangkapan Satu, etc. throughout the core system. This allows a pesilat to be able to instantly reference their hand and leg position and know what methods are available from their respective positions. This offers great flexibility and learning potential because the pesilat always has a point of reference to begin the next technique or element. To use a modern reference, Combat Silat is a GPS system for fighting combat. This is reflected in one of our aliran credos; Langkah dari batu ke batu or stepping from stone to stone.

As a pesilat continues throughout the core system, each new level of learning adds one more link to the chain. For instance, the third level of the system is Tangkapan. This is where the student begins learning how to counter if a hand entry fails to hit its target. They begin as they always have, utilizing the same eight Ales and all previous Masukan, they learn to check an adversary's free hand, pass from inside to outside and outside to inside, catch from all core Ales, and finally to trap. All of which use a corresponding numerical system. For instance, Ales Satu corresponds to Pencegah Tangan Satu, Pertukaran Satu, Tangkapan Satu, and Penjebakan Satu. To use an analogy, it is similar to the approach of building. You first start with the foundation, next the walls, roof, electrical, plumbing, windows, doors and finally, paint.

This takes place all the way through the system. As a result, the structure of Combat Silat is simple to learn and quickly brings pesilat (students of silat) up to combat speed.

However, the numbering system is just a method for learning. Later, the Combat Silat system really begins to shine when the pesilat begin mixing the numbers, i.e., doing Hand Entry One with Leg Entry Five. Additionally, modules may be skipped entirely. This opens up completely new territories of material for the practitioners to explore. Further, the jurus-jurus of Combat Silat take that a step further and give you a tool for extracting new techniques through the study of the movements of the jurus-jurus and the combinations of parts of jurus-jurus put together.

It is also important to understand that all the materials taught are foundational materials. In other words, a pesilat studying Level 7 (Tingkat Tujuh) is really only learning the most basic of material for that level. None of the levels are "advanced," but rather; teach a limited set of introductory materials about a given subject. Why not teach advanced materials as a student advances? Advanced materials are largely not necessary in combat and a student, once they have the understanding of the foundational elements, should be able to "find" advanced methods through their own study and thereby personalize Pencak Silat Pertempuran. For instance, I primarily teach a basic set of bent arm lever Kuncian (see the Chapter on Kuncian). However, there are many more kuncian that can be learned or taught and the pesilat should, once they have the basic tools, be able to discover many more or add them to the foundation they already have if they choose to.

Lastly, though a pesilat can develop quick combat skills, using our training methods of bunga and permainan a pesilat has the opportunity to increase in their depth of skill indefinitely. (See the Chapter on Seni.)

2a: Categories of Study

The core categories of study available in Pencak Silat Pertempuran are: Empty Hands, Weapons, and Ground Fighting.

These three core categories are broken into smaller areas of study. These include:

- Anfal Dasar (Basics)
- Ales (Evasion)
- Masukan (Entries)
- Tangkapan (Catching)
- Kuncian (Locking)
- Timbilan (Takedowns)
- Totokan (Destructions)
- Pembasmian (Eradication)
- Harimau (Ground Fighting)
- Langkah (Stepping)
- Jurus-jurus (Movements)
- Bunga (Flower)
- Latihan Berpasangan (Partner Drills)

Within these categories are sub-categories of study, which include a wide variety for the pesilat. Following is just a portion:

Anfal Dasar

- Pukulan (Punches)
- Siku (Elbows)
- Tangkap (Open Hand)
- Lutut (Knees)
- Sepak (Kicks)

Ales

- Ales Badan (Body Evasion)
- Ales Kepala (Head Evasion)
- Ales Harimau (Spec. Evasion)

Masukan

- Masukan Tangan
- Masukan Kaki
- Masukan Lutut
- Masukan Siku
- Masukan Sepak

Jurus-jurus

- Jurus-jurus Tangan
- Jurus-jurus Harimau
- Jurus-jurus Senjata

Tangkapan

- Tangkapan
- Pencegah Tangan
- Pertukaran
- Penjebakan

Timbilan

- Timbilan Tangan
- Timbilan Kaki
- Timbilan Harimau
- Timbilan Senjata

Kuncian

- Kuncian Tangan
- Kuncian Harimau
- Kuncian Senjata

2b: Stances Discussed

Notice that there is no mention of stances. In Pencak Silat Pertempuran we do not utilize "standing" postures except as transitions to further technique. It is our belief that "stances" are of limited value in combat – that is not to say valueless, but of less value than movement itself. The majority of people need more training in body mobility and fluidity than anything else. To then train them in the use of stances will only reinforce an already strong tendency of immobility. We do still utilize the specific postures such as: Kuda-kuda Tinggi, Kuda-kuda Menengah, Kuda-kuda Rendah, Kuda-kuda Bangau, Kuda-kuda Kucing, Kuda-kuda Monyet, Kuda-kuda Kalong, etc., but only as a secondary or tirtiary component at best. However, the use of these postures is primarily for communication purposes since there are few opportunities to ever "stand" in personal combat.

Additionally, we do utilize the various stances as opportunities for leg strengthening, and balance building exercises.

Section 3: Structural Philosophy

Combat Silat was founded upon the idea of principles, positions, and movements or mechanics. Ultimately we believe that All movements can and do have an appropriate use in combat. It is only when we try to define how those movements should be used that we often reduce the usefulness of the movements themselves, not because the movement is changed, but because we often lock ourselves into a specific use for those movements in relationship with our adversary. However, through the study of the principles, positions, and movements we may find seemingly endless technique, thus, my love affair with Pencak Silat. Generally, in Pencak Silat you are encouraged not to view movement in a singular fashion, but rather, to view movement as movement only and in co-ordination with principles and positions. Thereby, through deep study, reflection, and repetition, uses for the movements will "bubble to the surface." This allows any pesilat continued growth and depth in the system though they may have formally "completed" all of the material in it.

To continue, Combat Silat is simply the presentation of those methods that I feel best exemplify the most common (and also the most useful) principles, positions, and movements or mechanics of Pencak Silat as I have studied them. In short, through the study of the aforementioned arts this groundwork was found.

For example, why is it that about 90 percent of the arts that I have studied contain a version of the Hammer Lock? What is it about the Hammer Lock that makes it basically, universal? Largely, it is because there are only a limited number of positions you can be in, in relationship with an adversary, and second because the body only moves, bends, twists, steps, etc. in so many ways. As a result, it is possible then, to map out or create a method, which addresses, simply, a majority of these possibilities through a process of reduction.

More specifically, Combat Silat is a method that addresses, in a simple format, those possibilities but allows the serious student any number of possibilities and depth in their study through this format. Beyond being a complete system and idea unto itself, it is also a very "absorbable" system. That is, that it can easily be added onto or into any existing style as an easily teachable format that allows a new depth of understanding to develop.

Section 4: Combat Style

Our combative style is aggressive or offensive and direct. Our goal is to quickly take over the timing of the conflict even if in a seemingly defensive state. We do this by the use of our Masukan, which immediately disrupt the adversary's structure and interrupt their attack and mental focus. At no point do we consider ourselves defensive. The whole of the Combat Silat system is an attempt to maintain an offensive attitude and tactics base even when being attacked.

To continue, we start training at the next level of combat. To explain, most systems I have studied started their training by teaching blocks and then counter strikes. Later, if you continued to train, you were taught to perform an Immediate Counter. This means that when an adversary attacks, you also are attacking. You don't block their attack and then launch your own attack. This, is simply too slow in most cases to be very effective. Doing so also works off the timing of your adversary. However, if you work from the Immediate Counter as a principle of combat, you begin to learn the openings of your adversary and can more effectively make use of them. Additionally, you can establish your own timing in combat more quickly. Therefore, Combat Silat seeks to start all engagements from the Immediate Counter principle of combat.

Section 5: Combat Theory

Combat Silat (Pertempuran) is a martial art, but its first requirement is that it be an effective system for use on the streets. As such, a focus of what we teach is Observation, Interpretation, Application, and Correlation.

Observation and Interpretation involves:

- Environment
- Threat Assessment
- Physical Attributes
- Mental Attributes
- Spiritual Attributes

Application and Correlation involve:

- Environment
- Technique

Section 6: Observation and Interpretation

6a: Environment

Environment is a big consideration as it directly relates to all other aspects of what we teach. Environmental considerations take into account terrain, location, and legal climate.

For example, terrain can be grass, gravel, pavement, wet leaves, snow, ice, hills, trees, boulders, guard rails, walls, street signs, chairs, tables, glasses, bottles, rain, etc. The list would be huge if we tried to formally write them down. As for location, it could be a state or country, bar or club, pool hall, gas station, etc. As a sub category of location the real consideration could be the concentration of people or the lack of people, law enforcement or lack of law enforcement and witnesses or lack of witnesses. These considerations all directly relate to the legal climate. For instance, "is this legal climate that is unfriendly to non-citizens or guests from out of town? Do they have special ordinances regarding use of force methods or a continuum that must be followed to avoid prosecution? Do they have special laws regarding weaponry and what is considered a weapon?" These are a few of the biggest considerations that a person must weigh in their mind. Of course the decision can be brought down to this one idea: Is it a large enough risk to either ignore these environmental considerations or do I use the lowest common denominator when dealing with all potential confrontations?

6b: Threat assessment

Threat assessment is about helping people to recognize when there is the potential for conflict and either how to avoid, redirect or confront the conflict potential. This is a necessary skill in today's litigious society. This not only helps you to avoid physical confrontation but it also will help you to avoid legal prosecution if physical actions can necessarily be proven as being a last resort on your behalf. Further, threat assessment allows the individual to approach each threat realistically and to potentially avoid over compensation for any threat. An example of over compensation might be to remove a gun or knife from the hand of an attacker, be in control of the situation, but use the gun or knife anyway. Sorry folks the law is clear, you will likely go to prison if you do such a thing!

6c: Physical Attributes

Physical Attributes is another large topic as it relates to martial arts generally and Combat Silat specifically. We want to train people to consider things about their adversary/adversaries... if time allows. The consideration of attributes will help you to begin to notice details generally and will aid in a general idea of how to defend yourself. These are not absolutes but rather they are just designed to give you a potential starting point when dealing with the unknown. Following is a list of Physical Attributes you should consider when facing a potential adversary: (Some can be known while others may remain unknown.)

HEIGHT - REACH

- Much Taller - Much Longer
- Taller - Longer
- Similar - Similar
- Shorter - Shorter
- Much Shorter – Much Shorter

WEIGHT

- Much Heavier
- Heavier
- Similar
- Lighter
- Much Lighter

SPEED

- Much Quicker
- Quicker
- Similar
- Slower
- Much Slower

WEAPONS (Bodily Weapons)

Feet

- Highly Preferred
- Mostly Preferred
- Somewhat Preferred
- Somewhat Not Preferred
- Mostly Not Preferred
- Highly Not Preferred

Hand

- Highly Preferred
- Mostly Preferred
- Somewhat Preferred
- Somewhat Not Preferred
- Mostly Not Preferred
- Highly Not Preferred

Other, (i.e., Elbow, Knee, Head, Shoulder, etc.)

- Highly Preferred
- Mostly Preferred
- Somewhat Preferred

- Somewhat Not Preferred
- Mostly Not Preferred
- Highly Not Preferred

WEAPONS

Knife

- Pocket Clip
- Belt sheath
- Pocket bulge
- Screwdriver
- Bottle

Gun

- Coat bulge
- Visible holster
- Ankle bulge

Impact

- Wrench
- Stick
- Bat
- Bottle

MOBILITY

- Highly Mobile
- Somewhat Mobile
- More Immobile
- Highly Immobile

ENDURANCE

- High Endurance
- More Endurance
- Similar
- Less Endurance

- Low Endurance

STRENGTH

- Much Stronger
- Somewhat Stronger
- Similar
- Somewhat Weaker

BALANCE

- Stable
- Somewhat Stable
- Somewhat Unstable
- Unstable

SPEECH

- Clear and Understandable
- Somewhat Clear
- Somewhat Unclear
- Unclear and not understandable

Some of these attributes are clear as to their meaning, but some may not be. For instance, balance and speech may not be clear, but they do in fact, have a place in the assessment aspect of combat. They may, tell you that an individual is in an altered mental state. This could be drug or alcohol induced, or it could be for medical reasons. Of course, these are physically measurable, but ultimately relate to the following category of Mental Attributes. (It is necessary to know why you responded as you did when speaking to law enforcement. As a result, be sure of your assessment if there is time so that you may clearly state why you took "that particular course" of action.)

6d: Mental and Spiritual Attributes

Mental and spiritual attributes can be the most difficult to recognize and therefore, also more difficult to take into consideration. However, it is a necessary component to Risk Assessment and therefore, Threat Assessment and every other aspect of personal combat. (Following are two categories that could readily be noticed as being related to the Mental and Spiritual attribute's of an adversary, but we should not forget, that these need to be assessed alongside of the Physical Attributes since many of those directly relate to the mental and spiritual state of an adversary as well.)

AWARENESS

- Highly Aware
- More Aware
- Somewhat Unaware
- Highly Unaware

PERSONALITY

- Highly Aggressive
- Somewhat Aggressive
- Somewhat Un-aggressive
- Highly Un-aggressive

To continue, when dealing with an aggressor that has yet to cause any physical harm it is necessary for you to determine just what the intentions of the adversary truly are to the best of your ability. You must know if they intend on killing you, hurting you, or robbing you as an example. Certainly if their intent is robbery it may be the best course of action to give the wallet or whatever to the individual. However, if you determine that they are intent on hurting or killing you or someone with you then you must determine that you are either willing or unwilling to let them take that course of action. Once you have determined what the adversary's decision and your own decision is. You must take decisive action that matches that decision, even if it means you do nothing but hand over your wallet. Whatever you do it must be with your fullest intention! This does not mean that you cannot change what you think the best decision is but only that any decision must be made with your fullest intention, even if only to change it later as your adversary's intentions become clearer to you. (It is important that whatever you decide to take as a course of action, that you remember the reason why you felt it was necessary to take it. This is more of a legal issue, but it may occur, that after taking a course of action, you may feel some remorse for it, or that you may wish you had acted differently. However, you must be sure to be confident about your decision and stand by it, even in the face of questioning and in cases of severe outcome, i.e. death, you must be sure to clearly and unwaveringly state that you felt your life was in danger.)

6e: Application

Application relates to being able to adapt your ideas in the heat of combat based on your adversary's decisions and or the failure or success of your own decisions. This can take many years of training to accomplish but you must accomplish it! If you cannot adapt physically and to some degree also mentally then you will likely be defeated as the chaos of combat unfolds. This typically relates to techniques or methods that you already have in your command. (In this regard, Pencak Silat Pertempuran is more easily adaptable than many martial arts systems because of its modular structure.)

6f: Correlation

However, that is not simply the end, you must also utilize Observation and Interpretation to notice when your Application must change. Together, this is called Correlation. It can be as simple as knowing where your left foot is in relationship to your adversary's or as specific as the distance between your head and your adversary's, etc. Without observing your adversary's body in relationship to yours you will always have to guess what the appropriate action should be. Sometimes, Correlation can be thought of as Improvisation. As such, it is that element, which allows us to take into consideration all that we know (Observation and Interpretation) in relationship to our adversary, and perhaps use a method or technique that is spontaneous and is absolutely the right movement, technique or method for the moment. It is not necessarily "accidental" but it could be unplanned or a technically correct action that was not formally studied.

Section 7: Artistic Basis

Combat Silat is a simply structured and easy to learn presentation of those principles, positions, and movements or mechanics that I feel best exemplify the most common and useful aspects of the martial arts. In short, Combat Silat is founded on a structure of principles, positions, and mechanics that the artistic elements only enhance. Additionally, because of its foundational structure, artistic style and elements can be readily added to Combat Silat without the destruction of the system, but as a method, that makes it personal and expressive. As such, though the physical and artistic foundation is based almost entirely from Pencak Silat, it could be an expression of Kempo, Kali, and Kung Fu or just about anything else.

To continue, Combat Silat contains artistically expressive elements that have been taught as elements of the various systems of Pencak Silat to which I have been exposed. These include Sumatran, Maduran, Javanese, Malaysian, and Filipino influences, though largely, many of the more apparently silat styled movement expressions stem from the Sumatran and Maduran heritages respectively.

Section 8: Rank

Rank is not as important as skill. However, rank is often the only way for others who are unfamiliar with our skills, to relate to us. It is probably the most often asked question I get: "What rank are you? Are you a black belt?" It is usually asked as one sentence without pause. To help address this I have created a rank structure that is simple but will help you to easily know how to answer this and similar questions. Additionally, understanding our own rank will help others from different aliran or different perguruan to relate to us.

Besides skill rankings there are also Colloquial Terms and Persatuan Terms.

8a: Rank Structure

The ranking system of Combat silat is fairly simple. Essentially there are only 4 major skill ranks: Murid, Pelatih, Pengajar, and Guru. What follows is the complete list of ranks associated with Pencak Silat Pertempuran:

- Murid Satu
- Murid Dua
- Murid Tiga
- Murid Empat
- Murid Lima
- Murid Enam
- Murid Tujuh
- Pelatih Muda
- Pelatih
- Pengajar
- Guru

Murid

Murid rankings with the number designation are simply a reflection of the level that is currently being studied or has not yet been tested for. For instance, anyone joining Combat Silat is Murid Satu, which could be thought of as being the equivalent of a white belt.

Pelatih

Pelatih is a designation for someone who has completed not only levels 1-7 but has also successfully passed the required test for the Pelatih rank. You cannot have the title of Pelatih without having completed at least levels 1-7. The essence of the Pelatih rank is someone who teaches the physical component of silat primarily with little teaching of the mental or spiritual. Additionally, Pelatih may be considered someone who is similar in rank to a Brown Belt.

Pengajar

Pengajar is a designation for someone who has completed testing for the Pelatih ranking and has gone on to study Harimau and at least two different weapons. This might be someone who is similar in rank to a Black Belt 1st Degree.

Guru

Guru is a designation for someone who has completed the requirements for Pengajar and has gone on to study additional weapons, foundation jurus-jurus, and has also studied the spiritual component of Pencak Silat Pertempuran, understanding where it is contained within the system. This might be someone who is similar in rank to a Black Belt 2nd Degree or higher.

Pelatih Muda
Pelatih Muda is an honorary title given to Study Group Leaders. It is not indicative of skill in anyway.

8b: Colloquial Terms
Colloquial Terms in silat are those terms that are often used in place of the titles that are normally used in more formal settings. For instance, it is common for a guru silat to be called Ba Pak or Pak instead of guru while training. Following is a list of Colloquial Terms used:

- Ba Pak / Pak
- Anak Buah
- Abang
- Saudara
- Saudari
- Ibu

8c: Organizational Terms
Organizational Terms in silat are those terms often used to bestow an honor on someone who holds a place within the organizational structure. They do not necessarily represent skill, but may represent a specific assignment or task. Following is a list of Organizational Terms currently used: Jagabaya, Amir, Prajurit.

Section 9: Uniform

As with most martial arts, Pencak Silat Pertempuran does have a standard uniform. This uniform consists of four primary pieces; a black shirt, black pants, sarong, and ikat Kepala. Additionally an Ikat Badan may also be used. Shoes may be worn but barefoot is the normal method of practice.

9a: Baju Silat

The black shirt and pants can be a Baju Silat or a t-shirt with the Combat Silat Logo on it and black karate style pants.

9b: Sarong

The sarong can be any color or style the wearer wishes and can be worn with the pleat either in the front of the waist or near the right hip (not on the right hip but in between the right hip and the center of the waist). Pesilat who are not yet instructors should not wear the sarong at full length but must keep the sarong above the knee. Instructors may wear the sarong at any length they choose. It is also acceptable to wear the sarong tied as a triangle with the knot on the right hip or with the knot at the center of the waist.

The Ikat Kepala is simply a bandana for the head and is normally around 30 inches square. It is worn in a basic manner similar to the normal way of wearing a bandana in the U.S., however; the tip of the triangle remains untucked. The Ikat should be black.

Black and white Combat Silat Logo

Chapter 2: History
Section 1: Influences

That there are definite similarities amongst the various martial arts can hardly be disputed today. With the influx of new media and methods for documentation of the various martial arts, this is even more readily provable. However, what is truer than the similarities, which are usually defined by the techniques or applications of systems, is the fact that, generally, martial arts contain similar principles, positions, and movements or mechanics. This is what ultimately led me to find a home in Pencak Silat and, in fact, it is this very idea that ultimately led to the creation of Combat Silat.

That said Combat Silat is primarily based on Pencak Silat Pamur, Pencak Silat Raja Sterlak, Seni Bela Diri Silat Jati Wisesa, Pencak Silat Raja Monyet, Pukulan Pencak Silat Sera, Hok Kuntao and various Filipino stick fighting methods. However, I want to immediately say, that the combination of these systems is not a collection of techniques, but an understanding of the relationship of principles, positions and movements and how they inter-relate, as alluded to above. It was not a process of collection or addition, but rather, of subtraction. To define further the contributions each art provided would deteriorate the necessary relationship of those contributing systems and thereby weaken the relationship of each as a whole in Combat Silat. Additionally, my study of the contributing systems continues, as does my research into other systems of Pencak Silat.

With that in mind Combat Silat is the product of over 16 years of study and research of what the constants of the martial arts are. Through various trials, errors, and insights, Combat Silat was developed. To be sure, it could not have been done but for the grace and mercy of God to expose me to the teachers and systems that he did. In no small part this includes, Pamur Silat, Raja Sterlak, Hok Kuntao, Raja Monyet, Serak and Jati Wisesa. Through the study of these systems I have been given insight into a method of silat that is, by design, able to be learned quickly and to apply quickly to the street but that is not technique based.

Again, the primary contributors to Combat Silat have been:

- Pencak Silat Pamur
- Pencak Silat Raja Sterlak
- Pencak Silat Sera
- Seni Bela Diri Silat Jati Wisesa
- Pencak Silat Raja Monyet
- Hok Kuntao
- Stick combatives of various types

I continue to study Silat Pamur, Silat Raja Sterlak, Hok Kuntao, Pencak Silat Raja Monyet, stick combatives, and varied other Pencak Silat systems.

Section 2: What is in a Name?

Why choose Combat Silat as a name? The purpose of choosing Combat Silat as a name was to convey the purpose of what I teach and to represent the majority of the ideas, and in fact, the originating thought that resulted in the creation of Combat Silat. The Bahasa version of this name is Pencak Silat Pertempuran. Pertempuran means, "combat with many". Combat with many is a representation of what the purpose of Combat Silat is meant to become for the pesilat who choose to truly study it for the long haul. Normally I use the Bahasa and English spellings interchangeably.

Additionally, from a spiritual perspective, combat is meant to represent the idea that we all struggle with our very nature. We war against ourselves in the struggle to make it through life in a meaningful and balanced way, trying not to produce too many casualties of spirit and yet not become a casualty of spirit either. In that regard, the use as I have intended it would be similar to the Islamic term jihad as I understand it.

Section 3: Lineage

The lineage of Pencak Silat Pertempuran is as follows: Guru Wicaksono, Guru Cruicchi, Guru Wiranatakasumah, Si Fu / Guro Molash, and Guru Hassan Ali Al-Ansari primarily. Each of these guru silat has contributed to my knowledge.

Guru Wicaksono, Myself, and Guru Cruicchi

Guru Cruicchi, Guru Wiranatakasumah, Myself, Dale and Darren

Guro Molash and Guru Cruicchi

Guru Smith, Myself, Guru Shaw

Myself and Ma Ha Guru de Thouars

Guru Cruicchi and Guru Muthalleef

Chapter 3: Adat and Hormat
Section 1: Introduction

Adat and Hormat simply defined in English are manners and customs, and respect and honor. Largely, what constitutes Adat and Hormat, as seen in silat, are defined by the cultures of South East Asia. In some cases adat and hormat is similar to what you might find here in the West, but some are specific to the region from which the particular art comes from and may even differ slightly from teacher to teacher. These seemingly insignificant issues can find the western practitioner in a difficult situation because we are often expected or required to adopt the values, ideals and customs of a culture that is foreign from our own and, here's the catch, without being told! Unfortunately, sometimes, this lack of understanding results in the separation of teacher and student. Furthermore, what can make it especially difficult, in some cases is the inclusion of religious customs, values and ideals in the adat and hormat. For some this is not a problem. For others, the ideas, customs, values or ideals of another religion may go against what they strongly believe. Because of this struggle, I have outlined the basic guidelines for proper Adat and Hormat for those of you involved in the study of Pencak Silat Pertempuran.

Section 2: Adat and Hormat Guidelines

1. When entering the sasaran you should berhormat. This is normally just the informal or simple bow of placing both hands together in front of the face with a slight bend.

2. Once you have entered the sasaran and performed berhormat you should then also offer salam to the senior most person first and then everyone else. This can be done with the simple bow or verbally, such as "selamat malam pengajar/pelatih/guru/pendiri" followed by their surname.

3. At the beginning of class, perform the berhormat resmi.

4. While training, refer to other pesilat as Mas
   _____, for instance Mas Darren. Using the term
   Mas is an act of friendliness and respect. It has no
   significance in regards to rank.

5. When training with a partner perform berhormatan. This is done by first doing the Simple Bow, then shaking hands (right hand first and then left) and then performing the Simple Bow again.

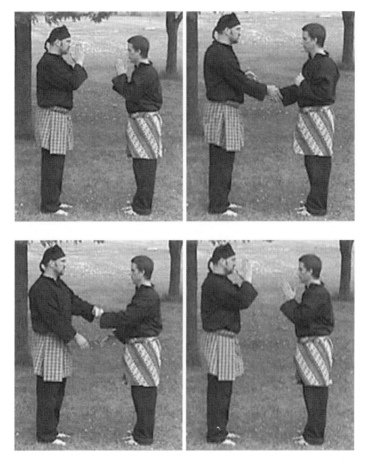

6. When completing the partner training, perform berhormatan. This is done by first doing the Simple Bow, then shaking hands (right hand first

and then left) and then performing the Simple Bow again.

7. If at any time during your partner training exercises you make accidental contact or otherwise break from the drill, it is customary to perform the simple bow as an act of asking forgiveness for the mistake or accident, you may also ask for forgiveness by saying ma'af.

8. Refer to a teacher in Silat Pertempuran as Pengajar _____, Pak _____, Pelatih _____, Guru _____, or Pendiri _____ for instance Pengajar Stark/Pak Stark/Pelatih Stark/Guru Stark/Pendiri Stark. Only refer to Guru Stark as Pendiri Stark.

9. When the teacher is giving instruction and or answering someone's questions, etcetera be courteous and pay attention to the information being provided. This will often reduce the number of questions in a class period simply because most students ask similar questions.

10. During the class, if you must leave for any reason, wait for an appropriate time and ask permission to be excused.

11. Be respectful in the sasaran. It is a time for all people of all beliefs, races, sexes, and nationalities to gather and feel welcome in the study of Pencak Silat. This includes the use of vulgarity, disrespectful jokes, etc.

12. Upon the conclusion of class, perform the Berhormat Resmi (Formal Bow).

13. Upon exiting the training area, perform berhormat by addressing those who remain and perform the Simple Bow while facing the sasaran.

14. When handling bladed weapons do not to touch the blade with your fingers.

15. When transferring a bladed weapon from one person to another, it is customary to hand the handle to the person receiving the weapon and generally a good idea to use the left hand to receive it. The use of the left hand is accepted because most people are right handed; therefore, this shows that you do not desire to attack. (This is a custom in the US only! In Indonesia the right hand should be used to give and receive. The context for this difference is part of a longer conversation...)

16. If receiving a sheathed weapon never remove the weapon entirely from the sheath unless the owner insists that you do. Only then, remove it slowly, carefully, and deliberately so that it is clear that your intention is only to view the weapon and not to use it.

17. Never step over a bladed weapon. Knives are considered to have spiritual properties in Indonesia and most other nearby countries and to step over them is considered an insult.

18. Never touch another person's gear or weapons without first asking permission to do so.

19. Do not pat or touch a person on the head outside of the context of martial practice. The head is considered the seat of the soul in many Asian countries and touching the head is seen is a sign of disrespect.

20. Avoid pointing if possible, it is not considered polite, here - there, or most places and depending on what finger you use to point with may change meaning, so unless you are sure, just do not do it.

21. Do not correct your instructor. If you think they may be teaching something incorrectly, ask them, but do so in a manner that is quiet and private. In most cases, you will find that there is a reason for any differences you may have noticed.

22. Do not change the material you have learned. It has been given to you in trust and with your interests at heart.

23. Though something like this probably should not even need to be said, do not even think about coming to class under the influence of drugs or alcohol. We use knives and other weapons and the things we do are generally dangerous. If you do such a thing, you will be asked to leave and not return.

24. In Indonesia, it is customary to bring white rice, a chicken and a burial cloth when asking to be accepted as a student.

25. To use any silat from a specific system it is customary to ask the Guru before using it and then it is normally expected that you would give proper acknowledgement of the material used when teaching it.

26. When referring to other teachers of silat of unknown stature always refer to them as Guru.

27. Be respectful of older brothers, teachers and all practitioners of silat. This includes all Aliran. Do not argue or debate about the effectiveness or ineffectiveness of your style or theirs.

The Golden Rule will take you far in Adat and Hormat. However, if you are not sure, it is always a good idea to ask. Most teachers will be forgiving and helpful if you show respect, humility and a willingness to learn.

Section 3: Berhormat Resmi

Berhormat Resmi is the formal bow of Pencak Silat Pertempuran. There is much detail to the Berhormat Resmi that is often overlooked and rarely explored. This section will be dedicated to the finer points, and meanings of Berhormat Resmi.

3a: Berhormat Resmi Described

Berhormat Resmi is divided into three sections, High, Medium, and Low respectively or Tinggi, Menengah, and Rendah. Each of the three sections has specific meaning and purpose.

Berhormat Resmi Tinggi

The high section of the Berhormat Resmi is designed to give honor to God. It is purposed for acknowledging God as the Creator and The Source of all knowledge and to give thanks for sending it to us. Additionally, it represents, in part, the contributions of Pencak Silat Pamur by including a portion of its Berhormat.

To perform the Tinggi portion start with your hands in the Neutral Position or Sikap Pasang Sebelas, then raise your hands to your forehead. Touch your forehead lightly and then raise your outstretched hands upward and outward. Return your hands to your forehead when you are done.

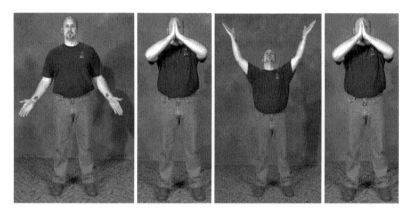

The middle portion of the Berhormat Resmi is designed to show our need for God to open our hearts by what we take into our mind. The connection is shown between our mind and our heart or our volition and emotions. It also represents the desire to be filled with Roh Kudus. Additionally, it represents in part, the contributions of various systems.

To perform the Menengah portion, start with your hands at your forehead, move your hands to your heart and touch them lightly to your chest. Immediately stretch out your hands to the front and outward. Return your hands to your chest when you are done.

Berhormat Resmi Rendah

The lower portion of the Berhormat Resmi is designed to show the desire to serve God with all of our being and to resist evil and temptation to death. It also has a secondary meaning of laying our life down for what is right and connects together the seat of our emotions with the seat of our desires. Additionally, it represents in part, the contributions of Pencak Silat Raja Sterlak by including a portion of its Berhormat.

To perform the Rendah portion, start with your hands at your stomach level and step forward with your right foot and kneel onto your left knee. Immediately extend both arms forward and downward to present yourself. Slap the inside of your Left wrist and then the inside of your Right wrist. Rise up to a standing position and place both hands together near your face and then back to the Neutral position or Sikap Pasang Sebelas.

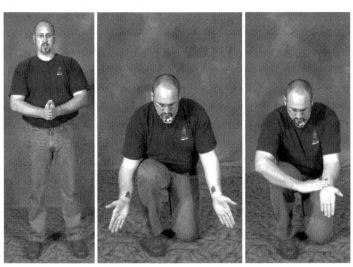

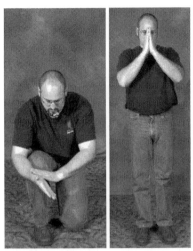

Berhormat Resmi Rendah

3b: Berhormat Resmi as a whole

Even with the various ideas that have already been mentioned, this still does not give the complete picture of just what the Berhormat Resmi represents. In addition to the spiritual, there is also the humanistic side, which is the three parts of man, Mind, Spirit, and Body. As well, they can be again represented as logical, creative, and needed.

However, there is still another characteristic that has only been explored a little and that is the cultural characteristics. The three parts each have distinct purposes for combat. The Tinggi portion is a call to God that our actions be just or true and available for examination by God Himself. The Menengah portion is an invitation to the opposing person, inviting them to "play." The Rendah portion is an assurance that you will lay your life down for what is right. In mock combat the Menengah portion is an invitation to play only and the Rendah portion is to show that you trust the pesilat and that you are hiding nothing.

In most cases, during the practice of PSP we will utilize the Berhormatan instead, but in a more formal setting the Berhormat Resmi should be utilized instead.

Chapter 4: Huruf
Section 1: Introduction to Huruf

Level 1 of Combat Silat is that part of the training which begins to develop the pesilat's "toolbox." The "tools" of Combat Silat are used as a method for technique communication, basic conditioning, evasion, and as methods for use in the application of personal defense. The study of them will begin the process of growth and development for further application down the road.

Tingkat Satu can be broken into four parts respectively, Anfal Dasar, Ales Badan, Ales Kepala, and Berhormat, usually just termed Anfal Dasar, Ales, and Berhormat. Through the use of the primary tools: Ales and Anfal Dasar, you will build your means of personal defense and that is the primary reason the level is called the Huruf or alphabet of the system, since out of its use "words and phrases can be formed".

Section 2: Pukulan (Fist Strikes)

2a: Primary Fist Strikes

Hammer Fist (Pukulan Tukul)

This is the primary fist striking method found in Pencak Silat Pertempuran. There is variety of reasons for this. First, it is a very strong fist striking method that allows people of various body types, the ability to inflict damage on adversary's, with less risk to themselves. (Largely, this is due to the musculature of the hand when clenching a fist.) Second, it is very easy to convert the Hammer fist into the use of many different weapons types due to the circular nature of the strike. Third, the Hammer Fist is primary because it is perhaps the most powerful fist strike and lastly, because it is very versatile in use and leads us easily into further techniques.

The Hammer Fist is formed by clenching the fingers of the hand into a normal fist with the bent thumb placed on the first knuckle of the index and middle fingers. To strike with the Hammer Fist, use the Pinky edge of the hand.

When training the Hammer Fist you can strike with one hand as a Hammer Fist into the palm of the other hand. This can be done near the height of the top of the head or low near the ground by squatting down on both feet in Kuda-Kuda Monyet (see the Harimau section) and anyplace in between.

In the photos that follow, three different methods for performing the Pukulan Tukul are shown.

Pukulan Tukul

Back Fist (Pukulan Belakang)

The Back Fist is formed by clenching the fingers of the hand into a normal fist with the bent thumb placed on the first knuckle of the index and middle fingers. To strike with the Back Fist, use the back of the knuckles and back of the hand area for impact.

When training the Back Fist you can strike with one hand as a Back Fist into the palm of the other hand. This can either be done near the height of the top of the head or low near the ground by squatting down on both feet in Kuda-Kuda Monyet (see the Harimau section.)

In the photos that follow, several methods for delivering the Pukulan Belakang have been shown.

Pukulan Belakang

Sterlak Punch (Pukulan Sterlak)

The Sterlak Fist is formed by clenching the fingers of the hand into a normal fist with the bent thumb placed on the first knuckle of the index and middle fingers. To strike with the Sterlak Fist, start with the hand horizontal and rotate the fist to the vertical position at the last moment of the strike, using the striking surface of the fingers closest to the knuckles at the base of the fingers with the palm oriented so the thumb is near the top of the fist, palm facing inward.

When training the Vertical Fist strike outward with the Vertical Fist as if striking something or someone. With the opposite palm, strike the forearm when the arm is fully extended.

Pukulan Sterlak

Pamur Punch (Pukulan Pamur)

The Pamur Fist is formed by clenching the fingers of the hand into a normal fist with the bent thumb placed on the first knuckle of the index and middle fingers. To strike with the Pamur Fist start with the hand in the position of an old English boxer and as you deliver the punch rotate the fist into the normal horizontal position. Use the striking surface of the fingers closest to the knuckles at the base of the fingers with the palm oriented so the thumb is near the side of the fist, palm facing the ground.

When training the Horizontal Fist, strike outward with the Horizontal Fist as if striking something or someone. With the opposite palm, strike the forearm when the arm is fully extended.

Pukulan Pamur

Uppercut Punch (Pukulan Naik)

The Uppercut Punch fist is formed by clenching the fingers of the hand into a normal fist with the bent thumb placed on the first knuckle of the index and middle fingers. To strike with the Uppercut Punch, use the striking surface of the fingers closest to the knuckles at the base of the fingers with the palm oriented so the thumb is near the side of the fist, palm facing upward.

When training the Uppercut Punch, strike upward with the Uppercut Punch as if striking something or someone. As the punching arm is rising upward, strike downward on the forearm with the opposite palm.

Pukulan Naik

Hook Punch (Pukulan Sabit)

The Hook Punch fist is formed by clenching the fingers of the hand into a normal fist with the bent thumb placed on the first knuckle of the index and middle fingers. To strike with the Hook Punch, use the striking surface of the second knuckle of the fingers with the palm oriented so the thumb is near the top of the fist, palm facing inward. Be sure you do not change the orientation of the wrist to align the knuckles; in this way your punch will rake the second knuckle of the fingers across the target.

When training the Hook Punch, strike outward with the Hook Punch as if striking something or someone. As the punching arm is about mid arch, strike the inside of the forearm with the opposite palm.

Pukulan Sabit

2b: Specialty Fist Strikes

The Specialty Fist Strikes are those strikes with the fist that are non-essential but in some cases, unique, interesting, and advantageous when used properly. The proper use is normally for those times when precision striking of a vulnerable point is necessary; as a result, they are often used as tools for Pembasmian though this is not necessary. Additionally, some of these fist strikes are advantageous when performing a Totokan.

Cobra Punch (Pukulan Ular Sendok)

The Cobra Punch fist is formed by clenching the last two fingers of the hand into a normal fist and extending the first two fingers, knuckles bent at the first and second joints. The thumb is curled.

To strike with the Cobra Punch, use the protruding knuckles primarily to hit/poke specific points of vulnerability on an adversary. The delivery of the Cobra Punch is typically done as a straight attack.

Leopards Paw (Pukulan Macan Tutul)

The Leopard Punch fist is formed by extending the all of the fingers, knuckles bent at the first and second joints. The thumb is curled alongside of the hand.

To strike with the Leopard Punch, use the protruding knuckles primarily to hit/poke/rake specific points of vulnerability on an adversary. The delivery of the Leopard Punch is varied and can be done circularly, upward, downward, straight, and raking across the target.

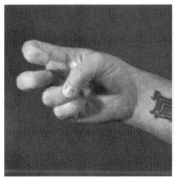 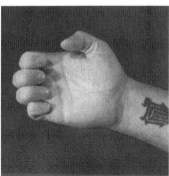

Pukulan Ular Sendok   *Pukulan Macan Tutul*

Scorpion Punch (Pukulan Kalajaking)

The Scorpion Punch fist is formed by clenching the fingers of the hand into a normal fist with the bent thumb placed on the first knuckle of the index and middle fingers.

Essentially the Scorpion Punch is similar to a back fist, but the emphasis on the striking surface and the method of delivery is different. To strike with the Scorpion Punch, use the knuckles at the base of the fingers to hit the adversary, using a whipping motion. The delivery of the Scorpion Punch can be done circularly, upward, and downward on the target, primarily for use as a Kerusakan.

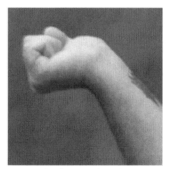

Pukulan Kalajaking

Monkey Punch (Pukulan Monyet)

The Monkey Punch fist is formed by clenching the fingers of the hand into a normal fist with the bent thumb placed on the first knuckle of the index and middle fingers.

To strike with the Monkey Punch, use the back of the fist and drag the knuckles across the targeted area. This type of strike is primarily a close range hit and can be done as a hammer fist, back fist rake, and dropping elbow simultaneously. It is range variable, meaning, that as an adversary gets too close it is the same motion as Siku Jatuh, and as they move further away it becomes a Pukulan Tukul.

Pukulan Monyet

Slap Punch (Pukulan Gampar)

The Slap Punch fist is formed by clenching the fingers of the hand into a fist with the bent thumb placed on the top of the index finger.

To strike with the Slap Punch, use the "heart" of the fist, essentially the palm, to strike the target on an adversary. The delivery of the Slap Punch is varied and can be done circularly, upward, downward, and straight onto the target.

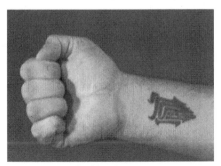

Pukulan Gampar

Clenching the fingers of the hand in an identical manner to the Slap Punch forms the Inverted Slap Punch.

To strike with the Inverted Slap Punch, use the "heart" of the fist, essentially the palm, to strike the target on an adversary with the hand inverted. The delivery of the Inverted Slap Punch is normally horizontal and from inward to outward. Often times used as a pre-cursor to a head/neck wrap or break.

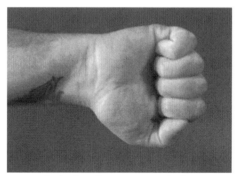

Pukulan Gampar Membalik

Section 3: Tangan (Hand Strikes)

The Hand Strikes of Combat Silat can be broken up into two parts respectively: Jari and Tapak. Many of the basic Tapak also include the use of fingers as methods of raking across the eyes and Jari Pecut.

Slap (Tapak Gampar)

The Slap is essentially a full, loose-hand slap on the target. Within the context of Combat Silat training, we also roll the palm over so that it can also become a finger rake for use on the eyes.

The delivery of the Slap can come from many different angles. The Slap is used on circular paths of attack.

Palm Heel (Tapak Tumit)

The Palm Heel is essentially a full, loose-handed Palm Heel impact on the target. Within the context of Combat Silat training, we also extend fingers so that it can also become a finger jab for use on the eyes.

The delivery of the Palm Heel can come from many different angles. The Palm Heel is used on circular path of attack as well as straight, upward and downward. Additionally, the finger jab can be used on the straight path and the fingers are kept loose. This differs slightly from the Jari Tombak, which keeps the fingers together tightly.

Knife Hand (Tapak Pisau / Papisau)

The Knife Hand is essentially a pinky edge strike, similar to the "karate chop." The primary difference is the use of slightly curled fingers.

The delivery of the Knife Hand can come from many different angles but the path of attack is on a straight trajectory and utilizes a rotation of the wrist. This makes it appear to many as a circular trajectory, but in fact, it is straight. This is in contrast to many systems, which use a circular path.

Tapak Pisau / Papisau

Back Hand Slap (Tapak Belakang)

The Back Hand Slap is essentially a full, relaxed, back handed slap on the target. Within the context of Combat

Silat training, we also "flick" the pinky fingers outward to perform a Jari Pecut with the pinky, for use on the eyes or other sensitive targets.

The delivery of the Back Hand Slap can come from many different angles. The Slap is used on circular paths of attack.

The following photos show this strike delivered in several different ways.

Tapak Belakang continued

3b: Finger Strikes - Jari

The Jari are those strikes with the tips of the finger that are non-essential but in some cases, unique, interesting, and advantageous when used properly. The proper use is normally for those times when precision striking of a vulnerable point is necessary; as a result, they are often used as tools for Pembasmian though this is not necessary. Additionally, some of these finger strikes are advantageous when performing a pre-emptive strike.

Spear Fingers (Jari Tombak)

As the name suggests, this is a method for striking with the tips of the fingers as though poking through something. Extend all fingers out fully being sure to forcefully squeeze the fingers together.

Primarily this is used to hit/poke specific points of vulnerability on an adversary. The delivery of the Spear Fingers is varied and can be done upward, downward, and straight. It is effective for use on the eyes, throat, groin, abdominal crease, and armpit.

Another variation of this is the Jari Tusuk. It is similar to the Jari Tombak but the fingers are kept relaxed and loose. Both are shown in the following photos.

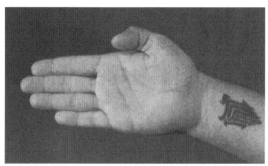

Jari Tombak

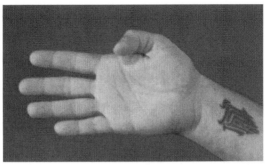

Jari Tusuk

Tigers Claw (Kuku Macan)

As the name suggests, this is a method for raking or clawing with the tips of the fingers on the vulnerable areas of the adversary. To form the Tigers Claw, simply imagine that you are trying to pick up a basketball using the fingertips alone to hold the ball into the palm of the hand.

Primarily this is used to rake, and sometimes poke, specific points of vulnerability on an adversary. The delivery of the Tigers Claw is varied and can be done circularly, upward, downward, and straight. It is effective for use on the eyes, throat, groin, inner thigh, chest, back, and face.

Boars Tusk (Celeng Taring)

Clenching the fingers of the hand into a normal fist with the thumb placed on the top of the index finger, thumb protruding, forms the Boars Tusk.

To strike with the Boars Tusk, use the tip of the thumb primarily to hit/poke specific points of vulnerability on an adversary. The delivery of the Boars Tooth is varied and can be done circularly, upward, downward, and straight. It is effective for use on the eyes, throat, groin, ribs, armpit, solar plexus, and inner thigh.

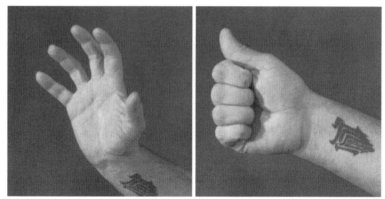

Kuku Macan   **Celeng Taring**

Section 4: Siku

Perhaps the most devastating of empty-handed techniques is the appropriate use of the elbow. To that end, Combat Silat uses the elbow for everything from methods of defense, attack, and for destruction of limbs. The elbow is largely used as a close-range striking tool. Primarily we prefer to use just the tip for making contact with the target.

Diagonal Elbow (Siku Diagonal)

The Diagonal Elbow describes and arch that starts near the waist and ends near the opposite cheek of the face. The back of the hand should brush along the face as the elbow is rising and remain close to the face and neck through the entire range of motion. This elbow can be used pretty much anywhere you see fit!

Downward Elbow (Siku Perisai)

Bring the hand across the chest and place it near the opposite shoulder. Let your elbow hang down in front of your chest. Raise your shoulders slightly, and then simply drop your weight as you also lower your shoulders. This elbow is often used as a Perisai since it is not extremely powerful.

Siku Perisai

Overturned Elbow (Siku Membalik)

Bring the back of your hand by the ear of the same side. Lift your elbow as vertical as you can. Slide the back of your hand down your face and under the opposite armpit. This elbow is very powerful and can be used when quite close, but is also more vulnerable to counter. This elbow can be used pretty much anywhere you see fit!

Siku Membalik

Inner Elbow (Siku Dalam)

Extend the arm as quickly as you can and strike the target with the inner portion of the elbow. This does not use the tip of the elbow, but the crook of the elbow for striking. This elbow strike is concussive and is used primarily on the head and neck region though it can also be used on the sides and legs of an adversary to upset the balance.

Siku Dalam

Horizontal Elbow (Siku)

The Horizontal elbow is probably the most common elbow strike in the martial arts. To perform this strike hold your hand near the side of your ribs, palm down. Simply draw a line across the chest with the hand, keeping the thumb in contact with the chest. You can draw the line above or below the pectoral muscles. If necessary the hand can travel into the armpit of the opposite hand or it can stay near the shoulder. Both methods are shown.

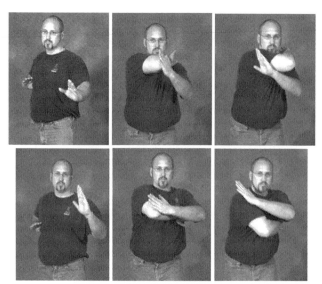

Siku Horizontal

Back Horizontal Elbow (Siku Belakang)

The Back Horizontal Elbow is similarly, very common in the martial arts. To perform this elbow strike start with your hand, palm down, in the opposite armpit. Draw a line underneath the pectoral muscles as you rotate your hand palm up. Your hand should maintain contact with the chest the whole time and stop near the ribs on the same side as the elbow being used to strike.

Siku Belakang

Falling Elbow (Siku Jatuh)

The Falling Elbow strike is started by raising your hand as high in the air as you can, palm facing outward, away from you, then, let your elbow fall on a slight angle towards the center of your torso while turning your palm towards you and turning it into a fist.

Rising Elbow (Siku Depan)

Place your palm on your cheek or next to you ear and act as though brushing your hair back. This starts the Rising Elbow strike. Continue to brush your hand back until the tip of your elbow is equal in height to the tip of your nose.

Be sure to maintain contact with your hand throughout the entire movement. This is an excellent tool to use.

Siku Depan

Section 5: Sepak

Combat Silat kicks can be broken up into categories respectively: Tendangan or heel kicks and Sepak regular kicks using the other parts of the foot, shin, and sole. This is the reason that there is a differentiation in terms. All kicks are considered sepak but not all kicks are tendangan kicks.

5a: Primary Kicks

Front Kick (Tendangan Depan)
The Front Kick of Combat Silat is a front heel kick. The method of delivery is to raise the knee up beyond the height of the target and extend the foot forcefully forward, striking

with the heel of the foot. It is not a toe kick. The mechanics are similar to stepping over an object. Upon completion of the kick, the pesilat should let the kick fall forward as if stepping. Use the hands to slap downward onto the knee to more forcefully extend the leg.

Tendangan Depan

Side Kick (Tendangan Rusuk)

The Side Kick of Combat Silat is a heel kick. The method of delivery is to raise the knee up beyond the height of the target and extend the foot forcefully sideways, striking with the heel of the foot. You should adjust the supporting foot by turning it sideways before kicking. Upon completion of the kick, retract the foot slightly, then let the kick fall downward as if stepping. Use the hands if possible to slap down on the area above the knee to forcefully extend the lower leg, as in the motion of a whip. This kick can also be performed as a stomping type of kick, which can include a slight jump. Both of these variations are shown below.

Back Kick (Tendangan Belakang)

The Back Kick of Combat Silat is a heel kick. The method of delivery is to raise the knee up beyond the height of the target and extend the foot forcefully backwards, striking with the heel of the foot. In order to make this kick more powerful, it is essential that we brace our hands onto our supporting leg, essentially performing a triangle with your upper body. With this kick, do not look at the target. Upon completion of the kick, retract slightly and let the kick fall downward as if stepping, then as the foot is planting, the elbow should rise to protect the head as you turn to face the adversary. The same kicking foot and elbow are used.

Roundhouse Kick (Sepak Bulat)

The Roundhouse Kick of Combat Silat is a toe kick. The method of delivery is to kick directly to the target. Very little emphasis is placed on having the kick be entirely horizontal. Normally the kick is delivered on an angle to a specific target utilizing the toe or shin of the leg.

To deliver this kick, shift your weight as though performing Ales Lima or Enam, on an angular plane, kick with your foot to the target in a circular motion. If performing this kick to the front, for training, rotate the front foot outward, into a type of gelek. Raise your knee on an angle and kick with your toe on a circular trajectory. Upon completion, set your foot down. Be sure to use the hands to slap above the knee to create whipping (pecut) energy.

Sepak Bulat

Chicken Kick (Sepak Ayam)

This is a slightly unorthodox kick. The motion of the kick resembles the scratching action of a Chicken, thereby getting its name. This kick is essentially a slap with the bottom of the foot to the groin of the adversary in most cases.

Sepak Ayam

Scoop Kick (Sepak Menyendok)

The Scoop Kick is also typically applied to the groin. The difference however, is that the toes are used to pull the testicles forward. To perform this kick raise the leg slightly, bent at the knee, with the ankle bent and flexed. Reach into the groin area with the foot, raise the foot up and retract the foot simultaneously. Step forward and down on completion.

Sepak Menyendok

Dragon Kick (Sepak Naga)

The primary use of this kick is to press the adversary's knee causing the leg to bend and the adversary to fall. To perform this kick, place your foot on the adversary's knee, toe facing outward (from your perspective). Press on the knee outward, causing the adversary's knee to turn and bend and forcing the adversary to kneel.

Sepak Naga

Front Sweep/Stop (Dapuan)

There are several ways to do the Dapuan within Combat Silat. The one shown here is just one. This is the most basic and simple way to do the Dapuan. This particular method is an extrapolation of the Sepak Naga. Other variations of the Dapuan include a foot slide, a baseball type of slide, and other variations.

Dapuan

The Specialty Kicks are non-essential, but in some cases, unique, interesting, and advantageous when used properly. The proper use is normally for those times when they can best be used to upset the balance or structure of an adversary. They are often used as tools for Timbalan though this is not necessary. Additionally, some of these kicks are advantageous when performing Kerusakan and Pembasmian.

Shovel Kick (Sepak Sekop)

The Shovel Kick, as the name implies, is similar to the action of a shovel. You might use this type of kick to "shovel" sand into someone's face... or kick him or her in the groin with your instep or shin. To perform this kick simply raise the knee slightly and extend the foot vertically in an arch towards the target.

Sepak Sekop

Python Kick (Tendangan Ular Sanca)

The Python Kick is a heel kick delivered by "wrapping" your leg around the adversary's and typically attacking the calf with the heel. Sometimes it is used to attack the knee or ankle as well. To perform the kick, place one leg behind the adversary's while facing them. Raise the foot in to the air while bending the leg. Forcibly bend the leg to strike the adversary's calf with your heel. This can also be used attack the inner or outer knee or thigh. This kick is an extrapolated kick from the Sepak Naga kick

Sepak Ular Sanca

Cut Kick (Sepak Iris)

The Cut Kick or Slicing Kick is a devastating kick performed to the ankles and shins of an adversary. Using the edge of the foot, slam into the shin or ankle in a slicing manner. When wearing particularly hard sole shoes this kick is nasty! The kick is designed to slice the adversary's shin or ankle using the edge of the shoe. In some instances, a person may even put sharp edges on their shoes or sharpen coins to use on the sides of the soles for this kick.

Sepak Iris

Section 6: Lutut

Combat Silat Lutut are simple and easy to do. There are only three, though there are many more ways to perform a knee kick. One key point to remember is to bring the target to the knee versus raising your knee to the target. Additionally, we use both hands to slap forcibly onto the knee when delivering and training the knee kick.

Rising Knee (Lutut Naik)

To perform the Rising Knee kick, raise the knee forcibly into the target. That is all there is to it.

Lutut Naik

Falling Knee (Lutut Jatuh)

To perform the Falling Knee kick, drop the knee of choice forcibly into the target. Gravity is your friend – use it!

Lutut Jatuh

To perform the Boars Knee kick, raise the knee on a 45-degree angle to the target. Do so forcibly as you pull the target into your knee and as you drive the knee into the target. This is excellent for use on the inner thigh, knee, and abdomen.

Lutut Celing

Section 7: Pernafasan

Additionally, to the basic hitting, kicking, and punching elements, many systems have breathing exercises. They have them for a variety of reasons to include: relaxation, power generation, spiritual development, emotional control, and even various forms of invincibility and spiritism. Perhaps this list is not even long enough to address every reason that Pernafasan are included in many Pencak Silat systems, however, it is sufficient enough to address the issue.

In Pencak Silat Pertempuran, there is no need for breathing exercises as such, since the Anfal Dasar contain all of the elements of training that are needed to increase power, speed, and intensity (our primary concern, and various other elements throughout the system address spiritual development, and emotional control). Essentially the Anfal Dasar, when performed correctly, act as Pernafasan, teaching us to control our breathing and how to generate power. Additionally, the Anfal Dasar cannot be performed properly without Rasa or spirit.

Proper breath control is essential in creating power and specifically the short energy of Pencak Silat Pertempuran. The key to developing the power is to utilize the entire body to generate it and understanding how the breath can impede or enhance that power generation.

Chapter 5: Ales
Section 1: Introduction

The primary thing you are doing is moving your body/head out of the line of attack. You are not blocking or parrying the attack and then moving your body. Proper Ales should utilize a body/head movement first, and then if necessary, utilize a hand parry, etc. if you cannot avoid it. Hand use should be secondary to the Ales.

That said Combat Silat is a system based on Ales. This means that all aspects of Combat Silat stem from the use of Ales. In all systems of Silat, Kuntao, Escrima/Arnis/Kali that I have studied Ales are essential. It is the basis for developing "higher" techniques and for reducing the factors of size and strength through proper alignment and angling. If your Ales are weak, it is fair and right to assume that your Silat will also be weak and ineffectual.

The Ales of Combat Silat are so important that they are taught on Tingkat Satu (level one) and are considered Dasar (foundation material). Additionally, Pukul, Tapak, Siku, Sepak, and Lutut are taught on Tingkat Satu as well. Be careful that you practice the Ales with the utmost care to perform them correctly and do not view them is simply a fundamental that, once learned, can be neglected.

What is unique about the Ales of Pencak Silat Pertempuran is that the Ales leave you in a position to immediately counter the attack. They do this because they are a method of evasion that does not necessarily require a range change. Additionally, the Ales do act as a power generator for your counter attacks.

In Combat Silat, there are eight basic Ales (we have a total of 12 that we practice). Be assured that in reality there are many more. The eight basic Ales use one primary principle... stationary feet. The eight basic Ales of Combat Silat are designed so that if your ability to move is impaired you still have the ability to evade. Think of defending yourself within a phone booth and this will give you our perspective on evasion. This does not mean that you cannot use stepping to evade. Certainly, you can and should... if possible. However, if the space you are in or other factors prohibit your ability to move freely, you should still have the ability to perform a simple evasion.

Ales one through four are designed for low attacks and Ales five through eight are designed for attacks to the head. Typically, we use the right straight punch as the basis for our Ales practice. You should also perform them against a left straight punch. Again, the first four attacks are delivered low and the last four are delivered high. The use of a high and a low attack represent the two primary zones of attack by most adversaries who attack the torso or head. Following is a listing of the eight basic Ales of Combat Silat and corresponding photos for the odd numbered Ales:

1.   Ales Satu (Arch Out/Side Step)

2. Ales Dua (Arch In/Side Step)

3. Ales Tiga (Turn and Tuck Out)

4. Ales Empat (Turn and Tuck In)

5. Ales Lima (Duck and Lean Out)

6.   Ales Enam (Duck and Lean In)

7.   Ales Tujuh (Turn and Lean Out)

8.   Ales Delapan (Turn and Lean In)

Section 3: Practicing

(Always utilize a training partner whenever possible while practicing any component of Pencak Silat

Pertempuran. This is the only real way of growing as a competent fighter.) When you practice Combat Silat Ales, practice with your feet stationary and also by allowing your feet to adjust in accordance with your Ales. Additionally, when performing the Ales, initially practice them without hand movements and later, after the evasion has been refined add the Ales Tangan or hand movements. In so doing, you ensure that your Ales are sufficient and that your hands are really only being used as a back up tool.

Additionally, though it is good to practice the Ales until comfortable only against straight attacks, later you should perform the Ales against various attacks to include circular hand attacks and kicks to the torso and head to fully explore them.

Chapter 6: Masukan
Section 1: Introduction

The Masukan of Combat Silat are the method that we use to orient ourselves to an adversary, they are essentially our Combat Positioning System. Through the practice and implementation of the Ales and Masukan, a pesilat can have a real ability to "find" their position and respond accordingly.

There are several different categories of Masukan. They include: Kaki, Tangan, Lutut, Siku, and Sepak methods. Through the implementation of these entries, a pesilat has the ability to not only "find" their current location in relationship to the attack and the adversary, but also through the study of the rest of the system components they can use this Combat Positioning System as a method to more easily find the "destination" or the end the conflict.

Often the term Masukan is used to differentiate between the specific application of a movement to "bridge the gap" or "enter" into an opponents space versus the general use of a movement without application. To clarify, the term Masukan Kaki refers to the act of entering the opponent's space by the use of a step. A step or stepping pattern is often referred to as Langkah. For sure, the steps involved in the Masukan Kaki could be considered Langkah. However, these steps are specific and purposefully created to be used as methods of entry into an opponents space and are thereby given the title of Masukan Kaki. The same is true of Masukan Tangan. These hand strikes are no more than Pukulan or Tapakan, and yet, when used as a method of entry to understand zones and control the space, the title of Masukan Tangan becomes an overlay. The same is true of all other Masukan. It's an expression or way to communicate the act of utilizing certain tools.

Section 2: Masukan Kaki

The idea of entries comes from Pamur Silat, which uses Masukan Kaki to enter or bridge with an adversary.

As with most things in Combat Silat, there are eight primary and 12 total Masukan Kaki. The eight entries are designed to give the practitioner a sense of location in relationship to an adversary. They also acknowledge the primary possibilities of leg positions in that relationship.

Initially practice should be performed against an adversary who steps forward with the right foot only. Later, practice the same entries against an adversary who steps forward with their left foot also. In addition, when beginning to train in Masukan, initially you should practice your Ales and add the Masukan onto it. In other words, your Ales are the beginning movements to the Masukan. Eventually when you are more comfortable the emphasis on Ales disappears and the Ales almost become transparent or invisible.

Masukan Kaki Satu

Shifting through Ales Satu, step forward with your right calf to your adversary's right calf as though passing by them. You should be outside of the adversary's right punch.

Masukan Kaki Satu

Masukan Kaki Dua

Shifting through Ales Dua, step forward with your left calf to your adversary's left calf you should be perpendicular to your adversary's centerline. You should be inside of the adversary's right punch.

Masukan Kaki Dua

Masukan Kaki Tiga

Rotating through Ales Tiga, step forward with your left shin to your adversary's right calf. This should be done as a jump with rotation but without a lot of vertical movement. You should be outside of the adversary's right punch.

Masukan Kaki Empat

Rotating through Ales Empat, step forward with your right shin to your adversary's right calf. This should be done as a jump with rotation but without a lot of vertical movement. You should be inside of the adversary's right punch.

Masukan Kaki Tiga   *Masukan Kaki Empat*

Masukan Kaki Lima

Performed similarly to Masukan Kaki Satu but utilizing Ales Lima. The primary difference is that you are now contacting right shin-to-shin with the adversary versus right calf-to-calf. You should be outside of the adversary's right punch.

Masukan Kaki Lima

Masukan Kaki Enam

Performed similarly to Masukan Kaki Dua but utilizing Ales Enam. The primary difference is that you are now contacting left shin-to-shin with the adversary versus left calf-to-calf. You should be inside of the adversary's right punch.

Masukan Kaki Enam

Masukan Tujuh

Rotating through Ales Tujuh, step forward with your left foot in front of your adversary's right shin. This should be done as a jump with rotation but without a lot of vertical movement. The final position has your calf against the adversary's shin. You should be outside of the adversary's right punch.

Masukan Kaki Tujuh

Masukan Delapan

Rotating through Ales Delapan, step forward with your right foot in front of your adversary's right shin. This should be done as a jump with rotation but without a lot of vertical movement. The final position has your calf against the adversary's shin. You should be inside of the adversary's right punch.

Masukan Kaki Delapan

The leg entries are such that you are either along side of your adversary or directly in front of them, behind their leg or in front of the leg. No matter what the case, you should try to enter at least at a 45-degree angle. On your "inside" leg entries your relationship to your adversary will be 90 degrees and on the outside entries your relationship will be in a straight line. The 45-degree angle comes from the basis that we start on a straight line and our adversary starts parallel to us. Once they attack, we will make an entry at

45 degrees in relationship to our starting point, which was parallel to our adversary. See previous figures.

To close, Masukan Kaki can have many different applications. It is therefore, necessary that you explore them to learn more completely what results you may have in a given position. For instance, if you enter with Masukan Kaki Satu ankle to ankle, you may find this position to be advantageous for sweeps, likewise, if you enter thigh to thigh, you may find this position more advantageous for certain Timbalan or Buang.

Section 3: Masukan Tangan

In street fighting, it is often the most difficult of tasks to safely enter into the combat range (or sometimes to stay out of it!). In Combat Silat, we place an emphasis on this entry whether it is by legs, hands, elbows, knees, etc. It is our belief that once a proper entry has been made it is easier to gain control of the timing and therefore, the combatant themselves. Through proper control of the timing/combatant, we are more able to control secondary attacks and or launch our own attacks. Furthermore, the eight primary Hand Entries or Masukan Tangan are designed to immediately counter an attack made by an adversary. It is not the typical block THEN strike relationship that is normally taught to martial artists, rather, we want to immediately begin to develop counter-striking abilities utilizing the weakness the adversary provides through their own attacks. As a result, we are more able to quickly and efficiently dispatch with an adversary because their own attacks and counter attacks offer us more opportunities for our own counters. Additionally, each attack by an adversary offers us yet another opportunity to establish our own timing/control, which further reduces the opportunity for an adversary to continue to counter attack. If they cannot counter, they cannot succeed.

In Combat Silat the Masukan Tangan do not focus on a specific counter attacking tool such as a back fist, rather, the tool itself is an option or variable that is determined by the pesilat depending on the outcome desired. For example, if a person attacks with a straight punch to my stomach I may choose from several different strikes. I may choose a Hammer Fist, Back Fist, Cobra Head, Knife Hand, Palm Heel, etc. Further, depending on what blow I choose, will determine the path that should be used for greatest efficiency and power delivery. Of course, whatever is chosen as the attack, determines the path of the counter, which determines the necessary timing and ultimately the outcome.

The Masukan Tangan besides being the hand entries of the system ultimately lead to most of the other facets of the system and should be trained diligently. The eight primary hand entries should initially be trained against a right straight punch delivered either high or low. The first four would be delivered low and the last four would be delivered high. Secondly, start by applying the Ales first and then adding the Masukan Tangan to it. Later make the Ales disappear slightly and eventually add the Masukan Kaki in. All number one Ales and entries should correspond at this point. For example, my partner might strike at my stomach with a right straight punch. I decide to perform Ales Satu (Evasion One) then I immediately perform Masukan Tangan Satu (Hand Entry One) and follow it with my Masukan Kaki Satu (Leg Entry One). This is the beginning of one chain. There are eight primary chains in Combat Silat.

As in the Ales, we train to enter off four low strikes and four high strikes. These four low and four high strikes are initially delivered in a straight line with the right hand only. Later, have your adversary attack with the left hand only and as you get more comfortable have your partner deliver hooking blows, uppercuts, rear hand jabs, crosses, back fists, over head strikes, etc. and adapt the eight primary Masukan Tangan to the appropriate attack, for instance, if a person delivers a right backhanded attack. Then the appropriate Masukan Kaki and Masukan Tangan would be numbers one, three, five or seven depending on the height at which the blow was delivered.

Masukan Tangan Satu

When your adversary attacks low with their right hand, perform Ales Satu while simultaneously using your Left hand to parry across your body while your right hand strikes the head.

Masukan Tangan Dua

When your adversary attacks low with their right hand, perform Ales Dua while simultaneously using your right hand to parry across your body while your left hand strikes the head.

Masukan Tangan Satu   *Masukan Tangan Dua*

Masukan Tangan Tiga

When your adversary attacks low with their right hand, perform Ales Tiga while simultaneously using your right hand to parry the attack while your left hand strikes the head.

Masukan Tangan Empat

When your adversary attacks low with their right hand, perform Ales Empat while simultaneously using your left hand to parry the attack while your right hand strikes the head.

Masukan Tangan Tiga   *Masukan Tangan Empat*

Masukan Tangan Lima

When your adversary attacks your head with their right hand, perform Ales Lima while simultaneously using your left hand to parry the attack while your right hand strikes their ribs or some other low target.

Masukan Tangan Enam

When your adversary attacks your head with their right hand, perform Ales Enam while simultaneously using your right hand to parry the attack while your left hand strikes their ribs or some other low target.

Masukan Tangan Lima   *Masukan Tangan Enam*

Masukan Tangan Tujuh

When your adversary attacks your head with their right hand, perform Ales Tujuh while simultaneously using your right hand to parry the attack and your left hand to strike the kidney or ribs.

Masukan Tangan Delapan

When your adversary attacks your head with their right hand, perform Ales Delapan while simultaneously using your left hand to parry the attack and your right hand to strike the bladder or other fine target.

Masukan Tangan Tujuh   **Masukan Tangan Delapan**

Section 4: Masukan Lutut

As with the Elbow Entries, the Knee Entries of Combat Silat or Masukan Lutut are designed to teach the student how to enter with the knees secondarily, but primarily they begin to teach the necessity for having a close range arsenal and targeting... for after the entry process. In addition, they begin to introduce the idea of destructions and disruptions.

The Masukan lutut follow the same pattern of entries for Masukan Kaki, Masukan Tangan, Masukan Siku, etc. and are easily learned. They same basic pattern is left and right knee from inside and outside of the adversary's arm. This only gives you four knees though. Well, they are directly related to the Masukan Kaki and can be considered a type of Masukan Kaki, therefore, if you perform the four knee blows and then step behind and in front of the leg after your knee, you now have eight knee entries.

When performing Masukan Lutut think of them ultimately as Masukan Kaki. Therefore when performing Masukan Lutut Satu, you should be able to end in the position of Masukan Kaki Satu. The Masukan Lutut are primarily used to attack the legs of an opponent, and are designed to break down the opponents structure and stability. These methods derive from the Boar (Celeng) fighting method. Although the Masukan Lutut directly descend from the boar methods (Celeng) of fighting, and as such they are for the destruction of the legs primarily, it must be said that they are not limited to targeting the legs.

Sometimes the need for a knee entry is not necessary if the adversary enters with his or her own attack or steps. At this point, you may actually use the knees as "shields" versus "spears" to use an analogy. Because the knees are used from the waist (not hips) down typically, they do not eliminate all "spears", except perhaps, those kicking attacks that are aimed to accessible targets. However, the knees will disrupt a hand attack through properly timed and placed usage, resulting in ineffectual hand and leg attacks by your adversary.

If you learn nothing else from Knee Entries, know that they are designed for close hitting and sudden defense.

Masukan Lutut Satu

As the adversary steps forward with their right leg and attacks with their right pukul, immediately perform Ales Satu and drive your right knee to the top of the thigh or ribs and step into Masukan Kaki Satu.

Masukan Lutut Satu

Masukan Lutut Dua

As the adversary steps forward with their right leg and attacks with their right pukul, immediately perform Ales Dua and drive your left knee to the top of the thigh or groin and step into Masukan Kaki Dua.

Masukan Lutut Dua

Masukan Lutut Tiga

As the adversary steps forward with their right leg and attacks with their right pukul, immediately perform Ales Tiga and start the rotation of Masukan Kaki Tiga as you drive your left knee into the outer thigh and step into Masukan Kaki Tiga.

Masukan Lutut Tiga

Masukan Lutut Empat

As the adversary steps forward with their right leg and attacks with their right pukul, immediately perform Ales Empat and start the rotation of Masukan Kaki Empat as you drive your right knee into the inner thigh or groin and step into Masukan Kaki Empat.

Masukan Lutut Empat

Masukan Lutut Lima

As the adversary steps forward with their right leg and attacks with their right pukul, immediately perform Ales Lima and drive your right knee into the inner thigh of the adversary and step into Masukan Kaki Lima.

Masukan Lutut Enam

As the adversary steps forward with their right leg and attacks with their right pukul, immediately perform Ales Enam and drive your left knee into the outer thigh of the adversary and step into Masukan Kaki Enam.

Masukan Lutut Tujuh

As the adversary steps forward with their right leg and attacks with their right pukul, immediately perform Ales Tujuh and drive your left knee into the outer thigh of the adversary, passing through with your foot and stepping into Masukan Kaki Tujuh.

Masukan Lutut Tujuh

Masukan Lutut Delapan

As the adversary steps forward with their right leg and attacks with their right pukul, immediately perform Ales Delapan and drive your right knee into the inner thigh or groin of the adversary, passing through with your foot and stepping into Masukan Kaki Delapan.

Section 5: Masukan Sepak

The Masukan Sepak or Kicking Entries of Combat Silat are designed to allow you a longer range starting point for an entry. They are used as a method to control and disrupt the base of an attacker and to enter while doing so.

They are not typically thought of as being an end in and of themselves but the beginning of further "entering" to finish what has been started though these kicks are potentially dangerous to the knee joint and can cause permanent structural damage to the knee.

Develop a high level of skill with these entries and you will not be disappointed by the uses you can find for them.

As for specifics, the Sepak Naga or Dragon Kick can be delivered with either foot to the inside or outside of an adversary's knee. For instance, if a person steps forward with their right leg, you can Sepak Naga to the inside of their right leg using the left foot and from the outside of their leg using the right foot. This is also true of the Sepak Rusuk.

Once contact is made push outward (or inward) on the knee joint causing a disruption in balance. Stay on the leg as you push and continue until you press the attackers knee to the ground. When practicing BE CAREFUL it takes a long time to heal the knee joints properly.

Masukan Sepak Satu

As the adversary steps forward with their right foot and attacks low, perform Ales Satu and place your right foot onto the knee of the attackers leg. This is essentially a low side kick or stomping kick. Press downward on the knee of the adversary causing them to fall as you continue to keep your foot pressing onto their leg all the way to the ground. It works best to brace the adversary in such a way that they are unable to step away.

Masukan Sepak Dua

As the adversary steps forward with their right foot and attacks low, perform Ales Dua and place your left foot onto the inner knee of the attackers leg. This is essentially a low side kick or stomping kick. Press downward on the knee of the adversary causing them to fall as you continue to keep your foot pressing onto their leg pinning their leg to the ground. It works best to brace the adversary in such a way that they are unable to step away.

Masukan Sepak Tiga

As the adversary steps forward with their right foot and attacks low, perform Ales Tiga and place your right foot onto the knee of the attackers leg. Press outward and downward on the knee of the adversary causing them to fall as you continue to keep your foot pressing onto their leg, pinning them to the ground. It works best to brace the adversary in such a way that they are unable to step away.

Masukan Sepak Empat

As the adversary steps forward with their right foot and attacks low, perform Ales Empat and place your left foot onto the knee of the attackers leg. Press outward and downward on the inner knee of the adversary causing them to fall as you continue to keep your foot pressing onto their leg, pinning them to the ground. It works best to brace the adversary in such a way that they are unable to step away.

Masukan Sepak Tiga   **Masukan Sepak Empat**

Masukan Sepak Lima

As the adversary steps forward with their right foot and attacks high, perform Ales Lima and place your right foot onto the knee of the attackers leg. This is essentially a low side kick or stomping kick. Press downward on the knee of the adversary causing them to fall as you continue to keep your foot pressing onto their leg, pinning them to the ground. It works best to brace or hold the adversary in such a way that they are unable to step away.

Masukan Sepak Enam

As the adversary steps forward with their right foot and attacks high, perform Ales Enam and place your left foot onto the inner knee of the attackers leg. This is essentially a low side kick or stomping kick. Press downward on the knee of the adversary causing them to fall as you continue to keep your foot pressing onto their leg, pinning them to the ground. It works best to brace or hold the adversary in such a way that they are unable to step away.

Masukan Sepak Lima   **Masukan Sepak Enam**

Masukan Sepak Tujuh

As the adversary steps forward with their right foot and attacks high, perform Ales Tujuh and place your right foot onto the outer knee of the attackers leg. Press outward and downward on the knee causing them to fall as you continue to keep your foot pressing onto their leg, pinning them to the ground. It works best to brace the adversary in such a way that they are unable to step away.

Masukan Sepak Delapan

As the adversary steps forward with their right foot and attacks high, perform Ales Delapan and place your left foot onto the inner knee of the attackers leg. Press outward and downward on the knee causing them to fall as you continue to keep your foot pressing onto their leg, pinning them to the ground. It works best to brace the adversary in such a way that they are unable to step away.

Masukan Sepak Tujuh Masukan Sepak Delapan

Section 6: Masukan Siku

The elbow entries of Combat Silat or Masukan Siku are designed to teach the student how to enter with the elbows secondarily, but primarily they begin to teach the necessity for having a close range arsenal... for after the entry process. In addition, they begin to introduce the idea of destructions on attacking limbs.

The Masukan Siku follow the same pattern of entries for Masukan Tangan and are easily learned. However, the value of the Siku should not be overlooked. Sometimes the need for entering is not necessary, if the adversary enters through his or her own attacks. At this point, you may actually use the elbows as "shields" versus "spears" to use an analogy. In so doing, you not only effectively "shield" yourself from incoming "spears", but you also damage the "spears" and eventually pass beyond the "weapons" to become the "weapon bearer".

If you learn nothing else from Elbow Entries, know that they are designed for close hitting and sudden defense.

Never use elbows to strike the top of the head, forehead or back of the head. You will likely cause permanent damage to your elbow and have little effect on an adversary. I have learned this one the hard way. If you use an elbow to the head target the facial area, temples, ears, neck, throat and base of skull. (Many of these should only be done in the gravest of circumstances - use with caution.)

The Masukan Siku directly descends from the monkey (Monyet) methods of fighting.

Masukan Siku Satu
As the adversary attacks your stomach area, perform Masukan Kaki Satu and right elbow strike the head.

Masukan Siku Dua
As the adversary attacks your stomach area, perform Masukan Kaki Dua and left elbow strike the head.

Masukan Siku Satu   *Masukan Siku Dua*

Masukan Siku Tiga

As the adversary attacks your stomach area, perform Masukan Kaki Tiga and left elbow strike the head.

Masukan Siku Empat

As the adversary attacks your stomach area, perform Masukan Kaki Empat and right elbow strike the head.

Masukan Siku Tiga   *Masukan Siku Empat*

Masukan Siku Lima

As the adversary attacks your head, perform Masukan Kaki Lima and right elbow strike the torso (typically).

Masukan Siku Enam

As the adversary attacks your head, perform Masukan Kaki Enam and left elbow strike the torso (typically).

Masukan Siku Lima   *Masukan Siku Enam*

Masukan Siku Tujuh

As the adversary attacks your head, perform Masukan Kaki Tujuh and left elbow strike the ribs (typically) as you pull the adversary's arm. Be sure to leave enough space between your adversary and yourself so that the point of your elbow is the contact area.

Masukan Siku Delapan

As the adversary attacks your head, perform Masukan Kaki Delapan and right elbow strike the ribs (typically) as you pull the adversary's arm. Be sure to leave enough space between your adversary and yourself so that the point of your elbow is the contact area.

Masukan Siku Tujuh   *Masukan Siku Delapan*

Chapter 7: Tangkapan
Section 1: Introduction

The Tangkapan of Pencak Silat Pertempuran are the method that we use to alter the timing of an attack by an adversary and to assume, alter, or change the timing and rhythm of the battle to one that is in our favor. Tangkapan as taught in Combat Silat is a general term used to describe a category of several different components, all of which are inter-related and overlapping. Each component is a variation of the others and is used as a means to highlight other possibilities for catching. The various components of Tangkapan are: Tangkapan, Pencegah Tangan, Penjebakan, and Pertukaran. Tangkapan can generally be used in either offensive or defensive movements since, fundamentally, there is no differentiation for a Combat Silat Pesilat. All movements are used with the sole intention of being offensive in nature.

You might ask "what the difference is between the various components of Tangkapan found with in Combat Silat since they are inter-related and overlapping?" To that, I might say, "Some of the difference is the mentality with which you approach the various elements." Let us take Pencegah Tangan as an example... In Pencegah, you can do them passively or aggressively. When you perform a Pencegah passively it is only a check, however, when you perform a Pencegah aggressively, it becomes a type of Penjebakan and can lead to further Penjebakan, Pencegah and Pertukaran. Additionally, the components of the various Tangkapan methods are an example of Pecahan. Pecahan means to break something apart or a fraction of the whole. In this regard, the various components are a breaking apart of the idea of Tangkapan, furthermore, Tangkapan are pecahan for the Masukan Tangan.

Section 2: Tangkapan

Tangkapan or catches are methods we use to momentarily catch an adversary's hand or arm. They are not meant to become power struggles between you and your adversary. Rather they are meant to cause a disruption in timing and the adversary's offense or defense as mentioned previously. However, if the Tangkapan become a struggle between you and your adversary then the question should be raised – who is caught? It does little good if your catching becomes a mental and physical struggle and you cannot break free yourself. So in this regard, Tangkapan are more akin to a Penjebakan versus using them as an actual hold or grip. This is one of the reasons why our methods of Tangkapan are not strong. We do not want it to become a fight of strength. The primary defining concept of Tangkapan in Combat Silat is the use of two hands to catch one.

Tangkapan Satu

Perform Ales Satu to avoid a low attack. Against a right punch, let your right arm "float" in front of the adversary, as though they are punching underneath your arm. Quickly clamp your right arm against your hip as you hook your right arm behind their right elbow from the outside of their arm. The fist of the adversary should be behind your right back/hip. Your left hand will come to rest on the top of the adversary's right forearm.

Tangkapan Dua

Perform Ales Dua to avoid a low attack. Against a right punch, let your left arm "float" out alongside of the adversary, as though they are punching underneath your arm. Quickly clamp your left arm against your hip as you hook your left arm behind their right elbow from the inside of their arm. The fist of the adversary should be behind your left back/hip. Your right hand will come to rest on the top of the adversary's right forearm or it can immediately perform Pencegah to the adversary's free hand to keep them from attacking you with it. This should be done as a mirror to Tangkap Satu.

Tangkapan Satu   **Tangkapan Dua**

Tangkapan Tiga

Perform Ales Tiga to avoid a low attack. Against a right punch, parry the adversary's hand or wrist with your left hand, into your right hand. Clench the wrist with your right hand. This is like clapping with your fingers pointing to the ground. Your left hand comes to rest on the upper arm of the adversary in a guard position. The free hand is kept free so that you can monitor the adversary's free hand.

Tangkapan Empat

Perform Ales Empat to avoid a low attack. Against a right punch, parry the adversary's hand or wrist with your right hand, into your left hand. Clench the wrist with your left hand. This is like clapping with your fingers pointing to the ground. Your right hand can come to rest on the upper arm of the adversary in a guard position or it can immediately perform Pencegah to the adversary's free hand. Your free hand is kept free so that it can monitor the adversary's free hand.

Tangkapan Tiga   **Tangkapan Empat**

Tangkapan Lima

Perform Ales Lima to avoid a high attack. Against a right punch, parry the adversary's hand or wrist with your left hand, downward onto your right shoulder. Simultaneously raise your right arm parallel to the ground and strike behind the adversary's elbow. Flex your right wrist so that the right hand is vertical. The fist of the adversary should be beyond your shoulder.

Tangkapan Enam

Perform Ales Enam to avoid a high attack. Against a right punch, parry the adversary's hand or wrist with your right hand, downward onto your left shoulder. Simultaneously raise your left arm parallel to the ground and strike behind the adversary's elbow. Flex your left wrist so that the left hand is vertical. The fist of the adversary should be beyond your shoulder. Certainly, you must be prepared to deal with an attack from the left hand of the adversary.

Tangkapan Lima   *Tangkapan Enam*

Tangkapan Tujuh

Perform Ales Tujuh to avoid a high attack. Against a right punch, parry the adversary's hand or wrist with your Left hand, downward onto your right wrist, as you simultaneously raise your right arm parallel to the ground and strike just behind the adversary's wrist. Flex your right wrist so that the right hand is vertical. The fist of the adversary should be beyond your right wrist. Twist the punch downward, slide your right hand down to the wrist, and grab it. Take your left hand and place it palm up underneath their right elbow. Certainly, you must be prepared to deal with an attack from the left hand of the adversary.

Tangkapan Delapan

Perform Ales Delapan to avoid a high attack. Against a right punch, parry the adversary's hand or wrist with your right hand, downward onto your left wrist, as you simultaneously raise your left arm parallel to the ground and strike just behind the adversary's wrist. Flex your left wrist so that the left hand is vertical. The fist of the adversary should be beyond your left wrist. Twist the punch downward, sliding your left hand down to the wrist, and grab it. Take your right hand and place it palm up underneath their right elbow or immediately Pencegah the adversary's left hand.

Tangkapan Tujuh   **Tangkapan Delapan**

Section 3: Pencegah Tangan

The Pencegah Tangan referred to as Pencegah, are simply checks to the free hand of an adversary.

In the context we are examining this subject, it refers to the hands of the defender, deterring the hands of the adversary for the purpose of reducing the risk of attack, counter attack, changing the timing, and control of the adversary. However, these are the "defensive" uses only. Pencegah can certainly be used offensively as well, to create a shift in mentality. For instance, when I utilize a mencegah action, I can do it in one of two ways. I can use it is a type of barrier that gets in the way once an action by the adversary is started. Alternatively, I can use it as a hit, which forces the adversary's arm to become the barrier to being struck. The method of delivery changes, as does the spirit of the Pencegah itself. Both the adversary and you will recognize it. Additionally, you can view all successful "blocks" by an adversary as Pencegah. Certainly, the adversary may already view them that way, but YOU can view them that way as well since you can determine exactly where the adversary's free hand is. Your attack simply became a Pencegah of the adversary's free hand which flow's you into your next attack.

It is important to remember that, Tangkapan methods are not the end in themselves, but a means to an end. Therefore, if it is possible to strike an adversary without the use of Tangkapan, do so without hesitation. Additionally, the principle that is being taught can be applied to any tool the adversary might use, using any tool that you might use. For instance, you may use your legs to check the adversary's legs or while lying on the ground, you may use your legs, feet, knees to check the adversary's hands, arms, elbows, etc.

3a: Pencegah Tangan Described

The Pencegah Tangan are simply a variant physical expression of the movements of the Masukan Tangan. To perform them, modify your Masukan Tangan so that your striking hand now becomes a precursor attack to the originating place of a counter attack. As a result, all of the Pencegah should target the area around the shoulder of the adversary's free hand, but do so in such a way as to cross the "zone" of the adversary's free hand.

Pencegah Satu

Perform Ales Satu against a right punch to the abdomen, letting your right arm stay in front of the adversary. Forcefully slap the adversary's left shoulder area with your right hand. Alternatively, you can attack the left side of the adversary's face by performing a Masukan Tangan, and if you are blocked, mentally shift, as though it were only a check.

Pencegah Dua

Perform Ales Dua against a right punch to the abdomen, letting your left arm stay in front of the adversary. Forcefully slap the adversary's left shoulder area with your left hand. Alternatively, you can attack the left side of the adversary's face by performing a Masukan Tangan Dua, and if you are blocked, mentally shift, as though it were only a check.

Pencegah Tangan Satu　　　**Pencegah Tangan Dua**

Pencegah Tiga

Perform Ales Tiga against a right punch to the abdomen, letting your left arm stay in front of the adversary. Forcefully slap the adversary's left shoulder area with your left hand. Alternatively, you can attack the face of the adversary by performing a Masukan Tangan Tiga, and if you are blocked, mentally shift, as though it were only a check. Be cautious on this move to protect your elbow joint from attack. One-way is to keep the elbow up above the shoulder of the enemy, another is to keep the elbow low and check with the back of the hand. Lastly, it is important to use great force when applying this or any check so that the enemy is "taken back" and unable to immediately perform a counter.

Pencegah Empat

Perform Ales Empat against a right punch to the abdomen, letting your right arm stay in front of the adversary. Forcefully slap the adversary's left shoulder area with your right hand. Alternatively, you can attack the face of the adversary by performing a Masukan Tangan Empat, and if you are blocked, mentally shift, as though it were only a check.

Pencegah Tangan Tiga   *Pencegah Tangan Empat*

Pencegah Lima

Perform Ales Lima against a right punch to the face, letting your right arm stay in front of the adversary but underneath their arm. Forcefully slap the adversary's left shoulder area with your right hand. Alternatively, you can attack the face of the adversary by performing a Masukan Tangan Lima, and if you are blocked, mentally shift, as though it were only a check.

Pencegah Enam

Perform Ales Enam against a right punch to the face, letting your left arm stay in front of the adversary but underneath their arm. Forcefully slap the adversary's left shoulder area with your left hand. Alternatively, you can attack the face of the adversary by performing a Masukan Tangan Dua combined with a Masukan Kaki Enam, and if you are blocked, mentally shift, as though it were only a check.

Pencegah Tangan Lima   **Pencegah Tangan Enam**

Pencegah Tujuh

Perform Ales Tujuh against a right punch to the face, letting your left arm stay in front of the adversary. Forcefully slap the adversary's left shoulder area with your left hand. Alternatively, you can attack the face of the adversary by performing a Masukan Tangan Tujuh, and if you are blocked, mentally shift, as though it were only a check. As with number three, protect your elbow from attack by keeping it pointing downward.

Pencegah Delapan

Perform Ales Delapan against a right punch to the face, letting your right arm stay in front of the adversary. Forcefully slap the adversary's left shoulder area with your Right hand. Alternatively, you can attack the face of the adversary by performing a Masukan Tangan Empat combined with a Masukan Kaki Delapan, and if you are blocked, mentally shift, as though it were only a check.

Pencegah Tangan Tujuh   *Pencegah Tangan Delapan*

Section 4: Pertukaran

The purpose of the Pertukaran is to teach the ability to continue an attack and to use what is given to you as the means in which you alter the situation. Menukar can cause a disruption in the balance and structure of an adversary and can thereby disrupt the timing of the engagement. Additionally, the exchanging hand methods can be further developed as a method to counter a counter attack by the adversary by utilizing the same movements but adapting them for use against the adversary's follow-up attack.

4a: Pertukaran Described

Pertukaran or exchanging is a method we use to go from over to under or from inside to outside of an adversary's attack or vice versa from under to over and from outside to inside, first performing a Masukan Tangan and then performing the Pertukaran.

Pertukaran are typically trained numerically from: 1-2, 2-1, 3-4, 4-3, 5-6, 6-5, 7-8, 8-7 However, this is just for teaching structure, the pesilat should go on to practice such combinations as: 1-5, 1-7, 1-4, 1-6, 1-8 etcetera. This can be done for any number, the key being, to exchange positions of attack, so a 1-3 would not be an exchange, nor would a 5-7 since they attack the same zone of target and from essentially the same position.

Pertukaran Satu

As the adversary attacks your abdomen with their right punch, perform Ales Satu combined with Masukan Tangan Satu. Immediately, using your right hand, scoop the adversary's right arm to your left as you perform Ales and Masukan Tangan Dua. The scoop is performed with the web of the thumb typically (fingers pointing down), though any clearing motion or tool can be used.

Pertukaran Satu

Pertukaran Dua

As the adversary attacks your abdomen with their right punch, perform Ales Dua combined with Masukan Tangan Dua. Immediately, using your left hand, scoop the adversary's right arm to your right as you perform Ales and Masukan Tangan Satu. The scoop is performed with the web of the thumb typically (fingers pointing down), though any clearing motion or tool can be used.

Pertukaran Dua

Pertukaran Tiga

As the adversary attacks your abdomen with their right punch, perform Ales Tiga combined with Masukan Tangan Tiga. Immediately, using your left hand, scoop the adversary's right arm to your left as you perform Ales and Masukan Tangan Empat. The scoop is performed with the web of the thumb typically (fingers can be pointing either up or down), though any clearing motion or tool can be used.

Pertukaran Tiga

Pertukaran Empat

As the adversary attacks your abdomen with their right punch, perform Ales Empat combined with Masukan Tangan Empat. Immediately, using your right hand, scoop the adversary's right arm to your right as you perform Ales and Masukan Tangan Tiga. The scoop is performed with the web of the thumb typically (fingers can be pointing either up or down), though any clearing motion or tool can be used.

Pertukaran Empat

Pertukaran Lima

As the adversary attacks your head with their right punch, perform Ales Lima combined with Masukan Tangan Lima. Immediately, using your right hand, lift the adversary's right arm to your left as you perform Ales and Masukan Tangan Enam. The lift is performed with the web of the thumb typically (fingers can be pointing either up or down), though any clearing motion or tool can be used.

Pertukaran Lima

Pertukaran Enam

As the adversary attacks your head with their right punch, perform Ales Enam combined with Masukan Tangan Enam. Immediately, using your left hand, lift the adversary's right arm to your right as you perform Ales and Masukan Tangan Lima. The lift is performed with the web of the thumb typically (fingers can be pointing either up or down), though any clearing motion or tool can be used.

Pertukaran Enam

Pertukaran Tujuh

As the adversary attacks your head with their right punch, perform Ales Tujuh combined with Masukan Tangan Tujuh. Immediately, using your left hand, lift the adversary's right arm to your left as you perform Ales and Masukan Tangan Delapan. The lift is performed with the back of the wrist and hand area typically (fingers are pointing up with the hand flexed), though any clearing motion or tool can be used. It is important to keep the right hand supporting the punch throughout the tukar to prevent the adversary's hand from hitting you.

Pertukaran Tujuh

Pertukaran Delapan

As the adversary attacks your head with their right punch, perform Ales Delapan combined with Masukan Tangan Delapan. Immediately, using your right hand, lift the adversary's right arm to your right as you perform Ales and Masukan Tangan Tujuh. The lift is performed with the back of the wrist and hand area typically (fingers are pointing up with the hand flexed), though any clearing motion or tool can be used. It is important to keep the left hand supporting the punch throughout the tukar to prevent the adversary's hand from hitting you.

Pertukaran Delapan

Section 5: Penjebakan

The purpose of menjebak is to teach the ability to continue an attack and to use what is given to you as the means in which you alter the situation. This is similar to the purpose of Pertukaran or Exchanges and though, Penjebakan can cause a disruption in the balance and structure of an adversary as well as cause mental panic, and can thereby disrupt the timing of the adversary as well as their mental state, this is not the primary principle. The primary principle of Penjebakan to be learned is the idea of "stone stepping". This means, learning the ability to be able to move from one position to another as if stepping from stone to stone to cross a river. Each obstacle presented by an adversary is simply another stone. "Langkah dari batu ke batu."

Penjebakan can be further developed as a method to counter the counter attack of the adversary by utilizing the same movements, but adapting them for use against the adversary's follow-up attack. Additionally, they can be used offensively to momentarily tie up an adversary's hands keeping one of your own free.

Lastly, Penjebakan can also be performed to the legs, utilizing either the legs or the hands to trap the legs. The Masukan Kaki are taught primarily as leg trapping methods unknowingly to the pesilat and it isn't until later that it is normally expanded to encompass a broader understanding.

Penjebakan or trapping are those methods which employ momentary "traps" of the adversary's arms in such a way that the adversary finds himself momentarily vulnerable to attack. Typically, this is done through various manipulations of the adversary's arms however it is possible to utilize other tools to complete trapping situationally. The primary defining concept of trapping is the use of one hand to pause / capture both of the adversary's arms / hands momentarily leaving the adversary vulnerable to attack.

It should be noted, that not ALL jebak utilize one hand to immobilize two. In some instances, during a jebak, the body of the adversary is oriented in such a way that it removes the threat of the free hand though it is not actually paused or captured. These times could be viewed as Tangkapan rather than Penjebakan, but the separation is semantic since all methods of catching, checking, trapping, and exchanging fall into the category of Tangkapan.

Penjebakan are performed by first performing a Masukan Tangan. If the attack is blocked you can then perform a Penjebakan. Additionally, traps can be performed when someone grabs you with both hands or, if you grab the adversary's free hand and manipulate it into a jebak.

The difficulty in Penjebakan and the principle of stone stepping generally is that often there are too many ways to get from one "stone" to another. As a result, we have chosen to limit what "stones" you initially use to ease that burden.

Lastly, any of the follow-ups could be substituted with Siku instead of Tangan strikes.

Penjebakan Satu

Perform a Masukan Tangan Satu, attacking the left side of the head of the adversary. The adversary will block the strike with their left hand. The moment you feel the block, bend your right arm at the elbow and hook the adversary's right arm, lifting it, as you rotate and perform Ales Tujuh with Masukan Tangan Tujuh.

Penjebakan Dua

Perform a Masukan Tangan Dua, attacking the left side of the adversary's head. The adversary will block the strike with their left hand. The moment you feel the block, use your left hand to tangkap the outside of the adversary's left forearm and attack the head with your right hand, essentially performing a Masukan Tangan Tiga (using the adversary's left hand as the reference point now).

Penjebakan Tiga

Perform a Masukan Tangan Tiga, attacking the face of the adversary. The adversary will block the strike with their left hand. The moment you feel the block, use your left hand to tangkap the left wrist of the adversary and attack the ribs with your right hand, essentially performing a

Masukan Tangan Tujuh (using the adversary's left hand as the reference point now).

Penjebakan Tiga

Penjebakan Empat

Perform a Masukan Tangan Empat, attacking the right side of the adversary's head. The adversary will block the strike with their left hand. The moment you feel the block, using your right hand, reach over the adversary's right arm and hook the elbow. Turn the adversary to their left and strike the adversary with your left hand, essentially performing a Masukan Tangan Tujuh (using the adversary's right hand as the reference point).

Penjebakan Empat

Penjebakan Lima

Perform a Masukan Tangan Lima, attacking the ribs of the adversary. The adversary will block the strike with their left hand. The moment you feel the block, circle your right hand outward and use your right hand to press the adversary's right arm across their chest. As the adversary is turned away, strike the kidney or ribs with your left hand, essentially performing a Masukan Tangan Tujuh (using the adversary's right hand as the reference point).

Penjebakan Enam

Perform a Masukan Tangan Enam, attacking the groin of the adversary. The adversary will block the strike with their left hand. The moment you feel the block, circle your left hand (suliwa) around the block and grab (tangkap) the arm of the adversary's left hand, pinning it against their body. Attack with your right hand to their left cheek, essentially performing a Masukan Tangan Tiga (using the adversary's left hand as the reference point now). Likewise, other traps could also be performed off this entry as well.

Penjebakan Enam

Penjebakan Tujuh

Perform a Masukan Tangan Tujuh, attacking the face of the adversary with a Pukulan Belakang. The adversary will block the strike with their left hand. The moment you feel the block, use your right hand to lift the elbow of the adversary's left hand. Attack with your left hand to their left ribs, essentially performing a Masukan Tangan Lima (using the adversary's left hand as the reference point now).

Penjebakan Delapan

Perform a Masukan Tangan Delapan, attacking the groin of the adversary with a Pukulan Tukul. The adversary will block the strike with their left hand. The moment you feel the block, use your left hand to tangkap the wrist of the adversary's left hand, grabbing their wrist and lifting upward. Attack with your right hand to their left ribs, essentially performing a Masukan Tangan Tujuh (using the adversary's left hand as the reference point now).

Chapter 8 - Kuncian
Section 1: Introduction

By now, a pattern should be presenting itself as you read this training manual. All elements of Pencak Silat Pertempuran derive from Ales Badan. Some are more clearly explained by focusing on the Masukan, but a good Masukan always includes Ales Badan first. Kuncian are no exception.

The basic Kuncian themselves are specifically taught and derive from the Ular Sanca system or Python. This means that the Kuncian are derived from the type of motion used by a Python. This motion includes a circular entwining motion primarily but also includes a twisting, compressing, and pulling facet to them as well. In addition, like a python, we do not place a Kuncian on an adversary unless we can also perform a breaking / dislocating (herein referred to as breaking) technique on the "locked" limb. The basic reason is that while we do not prefer to harm an adversary we have chosen to Kuncian, it is sometimes necessary for our own safety or the safety of someone else. As an example, although it's not preferred, in a situation where you are forced into the disadvantaged situation of dealing with multiple adversary's, it may be necessary to break an adversary's limb versus locking it in order to be free to defend against further attacks from the remaining adversary's.

Within the system, there are MANY more possibilities for kuncian, some of which come from the Harimau Subsystem of ground fighting and will be covered within the context of that material. You are not limited by what is taught but by what you can imagine.

1a: Kuncian Described

Kuncian are a means of gaining advantage on an adversary by specifically targeting a joint or joints of the adversary through bending, straightening, or twisting in such a way as to gain control of the adversary with the option of minimizing the necessity to severely hurt the adversary. A properly applied Kuncian has the ability to separate the joint causing dislocation, and tearing of the ligaments, tendons, and muscles.

To apply the locks of the Ular Sanca system you must learn to flow into them out of your Masukan. Rarely will the opportunity present itself that you can just apply a kuncian without first distracting an adversary. Further, kuncian should be applied quickly and with sharp power to reduce the possibility of resistance by disrupting the adversary's balance or center of gravity. If resistance is met at any stage of a kuncian it is often better to re-distract, follow the energy and apply a different kuncian, or forget the kuncian altogether.

Further, the best Kuncian, contain two general aspects to them: one is Pain Control and the other is Structural

Control. The Structural Control Kuncian, are those Kuncian which, restrict the movement of an individual through structural control. The Pain Control Kuncian is a Kuncian, which restricts movement through the production of pain. Interestingly, you can have Structural Control without Pain Control but you cannot have Pain Control without Structural Control. In Combat Silat, we prefer to have both Structural and Pain Control Kuncian. If you choose to perform a Structural Control Kuncian without a Pain Control aspect, the adversary will likely fight against the lock and your control through Kuncian will be brief.

To expand a bit on Pain Control Kuncian it is necessary to have one of two aspects: hyperextension or hyperflexion. Additionally, to further increase the effectiveness of either hyperextension or hyperflexion it is useful to add rotation to the joint as well. Additionally, in order to have Pain Control Kuncian, it is not always necessary to apply it to the joint actually being locked. It is possible to apply the pain control to a pressure point in such a way as to maintain a Structural Control Kuncian.

Finally, please remember YOU DO NOT HAVE TO APPLY ANY KUNCIAN – EVER! Kuncian are strictly a method to control and show mercy.

Kuncian Satu

Perform Masukan Tangan Satu against a low attack. With your right arm over the adversary's right arm, step forward into Masukan Kaki Satu as you drive your right shoulder into the upper arm of the adversary's right arm. Using the back of your left hand, press the adversary's right arm down and backward until you turn your left hand palm up. Using your right hand, grab the adversary's right hand and flex the wrist by bending it acutely upward or downward. At this point you can either switch the hand that is doing the lock, or stay as you are. If you do not switch, utilizing your left hand reach around the adversary's head and using the pressure point underneath the left side of the jaw of the adversary, cause their head to tip backward. If you do switch, use your right hand to reach around the adversary's head and using the pressure point underneath the jaw of the adversary, cause their head to tip backward. Additional variations exist by the handful. CAUTION: The adversary can still kick you in the groin and shins. (The lock is shown with a Left lead below instead of a right lead.)

Kuncian Satu

Kuncian Dua

Perform Masukan Tangan Dua against a low attack. With your left arm over the adversary's right arm, perform a counter-clockwise circle. Use your right hand to control the hand of the adversary's right arm. Press downward onto the inner elbow of the adversary's right arm with your left palm to cause the their arm to bend. Continue to circle your left arm in a counter-clockwise circle. Using both hands, lift the bent arm of the adversary causing stress to the shoulder. Additional variations exist. CAUTION: The adversary may still able to strike you with their free hand.

It is often the case that as the adversary draws their hand back they will make the lock easier to obtain. Additionally, if the adversary strikes at your head with their left hand, perform Ales Tujuh and parry their left hand over their right arm and use your elbow to apply pressure, holding both hands with one lock.

Kuncian Dua

Kuncian Tiga

Perform Masukan Tangan Tiga against a low attack. With your left arm over the adversary's right arm, perform a clockwise circle. Use your left hand to press against the crook of their elbow, causing the arm to bend. Use your right hand to control the hand of the adversary's right arm. Roll the adversary's elbow clockwise causing their arm to bend at the elbow. Pull the adversary's elbow to your chest with both hands. This should cause the adversary to bend over at the waist. Additionally, once the adversary is bent over, you may also use the right hand to press pressure points on the face, causing the opponent to stand upright. This will help to prevent some counter kuncian movements.

Continued...

Kuncian Tiga

Kuncian Empat

Perform Masukan Tangan Empat against a low attack. With your right arm over the adversary's right arm, use your left hand to place their wrist into your right armpit. Circle your arm counter-clockwise until you are able to grab the adversary's throat. Do not release the hand that is trapped in your armpit. Using your left hand reach behind the adversary's neck and clasp your right and left hands together. Additional variations exist.

Kuncian Empat

Kuncian Lima

As the attack comes to your head, utilize your right elbow to parry the punch outward and perform a counterclockwise wrap with your right elbow. With your right arm over the adversary's right arm, use your left hand to place their wrist into your right armpit. Circle your arm counter-clockwise until you are able to grab the adversary's throat. Do not release the hand that is trapped in your armpit. Using your left hand reach behind the adversary's neck and clasp your right and left hands together. Additional variations exist. This is an identical technique to Kuncian Empat but starts from a different attack.

Kuncian Lima

Kuncian Enam

As the attack comes to your head, utilize your left elbow to parry the punch inward and perform a clockwise wrap with your left elbow. Use your right hand to control the hand of the adversary's right arm. Roll the adversary's elbow causing their arm to bend at the elbow. Pull the adversary's elbow to your chest with both hands. This should cause the adversary to bend over at the waist. Using both hands, lift the bent arm of the adversary causing stress to the shoulder. Use the right hand to grab the fingers of the adversary and bend them acutely causing a finger lock and potentially a wristlock. Additional variations exist. CAUTION: The adversary may still able to strike you with their free hand to the groin and abdominal area. This is an identical technique to Kuncian Tiga but starts from an attack to the head.

Continued...

Kuncian Enam

Kuncian Tujuh

Perform Masukan Tangan Tujuh against a high attack. With your left arm under the adversary's right arm, and your right hand holding the adversary's right hand in place, use your left forearm to pull/rub the adversary's elbow causing their arm to bend. Once their arm is bent, place the wrist of the adversary into the crook of your left elbow, and pull with both hands, drawing the adversary's elbow towards you. It should end similarly in appearance to Kuncian Tiga.

Alternately, you may perform a compressing wristlock by drawing back on the inside of the elbow with your right hand, causing the elbow to bend. Be sure to tuck the elbow into your under arm area and with your left hand begin to apply pressure on the adversary's hand causing their wrist to bend. Immediately grab their hand with both hands and press.

Alternate Kuncian Tujuh

Kuncian Delapan

Perform Masukan Tangan Delapan against a high attack. With your right arm under the adversary's right arm, reach up and pull down in the bend of the adversary's arm. Immediately shoot your right hand up and grab the right wrist of the adversary. Pull down with both hands while lifting with your right forearm, creating a fulcrum point slightly nearer the adversary's shoulder, beyond their elbow. Try to get the adversary to stand on their tiptoes. This is normally referred to as a "Hammer Lock." Additional variations exist. CAUTION: The adversary can still sometimes strike you with their free hand to the head and abdominal area. They may also be able to knee or kick.

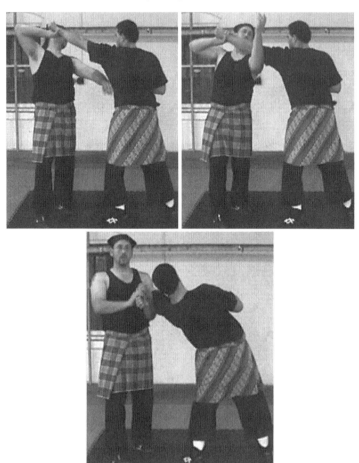

Chapter 9: Timbilan
Section 1: Introduction

Timbilan are sometimes referred to as Buang in some silat systems. Essentially, no matter how you might say it, the meaning is to perform takedowns or throws on the adversary.

The methods of Timbilan found in Pencak Silat Pertempuran are a product of the reference system created by the various Ales and Masukan of the system. The core Timbilan that are trained teach principles with many variations. This is not to say that there are not many more takedowns or throws which could be utilized in their place. The serious pesilat should consider learning various takedowns from every lock and every entry as well.

Section 2: Timbilan Described

The purpose of the Timbilan as performed within Pencak Silat Pertempuran is to remove the opponent from the action of combat in such a way that they have difficulty recovering. Timbilan can be broken up into different categories, for instance, Timbilan Tangan and Timbilan Kaki. These two categories comprise the whole of the throwing methods found in Combat Silat and reference the primary tool the pesilat will use when accomplishing the various takedowns or throws on the adversary.

When throwing or taking down it is often the goal to harm the adversary that you are performing the technique on, rarely is it the goal to gently let the opponent fall. This is especially true in Pencak Silat generally. Many of the takedowns do not gracefully lend themselves to the break falls so commonly seen in other martial arts. In fact, it is often said by the "players" themselves, that it is impossible to break fall from the majority of Timbilan found in Combat Silat.

2a: Timbilan Kaki Described

Timbilan Kaki refers to any takedown or throw that utilizes the legs as the primary tool of the Timbilan. Largely, these are sweeps, though they can include kneeling, and tripping methods as well. For the sake of Combat Silat, the primary method is sweeping with the foot from the position of a Masukan Kaki.

Timbilan Kaki Satu

This sweep utilizes opposing force on the upper and lower body. Step behind the adversary's right foot with your right foot, utilizing Masukan Kaki Satu. Once your feet are settled, slide your right foot backward to cause their right foot to slide. Simultaneously use your right hand or arm to block the front of their right shoulder to keep their upper body from moving in the direction of the sweep, forcing the adversary to fall onto their buttocks.

Timbilan Kaki Dua

This sweep utilizes opposing force on the upper and lower body. Step behind the adversary's right foot with your left foot, utilizing Masukan Kaki Dua. Once your feet are settled, slide your left foot backward to cause their foot to move. Simultaneously use your left hand or arm to gently push downward and forward on the shoulder to force the adversary to fall onto their face. Alternatively it is possible to make the adversary fall on their buttocks but it is more difficult.

Timbilan Kaki Tiga

This sweep utilizes opposing force on the upper and lower body. Step behind the adversary's right foot with your left foot, utilizing Masukan Kaki Tiga. Once your feet are settled, slide your left foot to your right foot bringing your feet together, causing their foot to move. Simultaneously use your left hand or arm to gently pull back and press down on the shoulder of the adversary causing them to fall on their buttocks.

Timbilan Kaki Empat

This sweep utilizes opposing force on the upper and lower body. Step behind the adversary's right foot with your right foot, utilizing Masukan Kaki Empat. Once your feet are settled, slide your right foot to your left foot bringing your feet together, causing their foot to move. Simultaneously use your right hand or arm to gently push downward and backward on the front of the shoulder to force the adversary to fall onto their buttocks.

Timbilan Kaki Lima

This sweep utilizes opposing force on the upper and lower body. To begin, step in front of the adversary's right foot with your right foot, utilizing Masukan Kaki Lima. Once your feet are settled, slide your right foot to your left foot bringing your feet together, causing their foot to move. Simultaneously use your right hand or arm to gently push downward and backward on the front of their hip to force the adversary to fall onto their buttocks.

Timbilan Kaki Enam

This sweep utilizes opposing force on the upper and lower body. To begin, Step in front of the adversary's right foot with your left foot, utilizing Masukan Kaki Enam. Once your feet are settled, slide your left foot to your right foot bringing your feet together, causing their foot to move. Simultaneously use your left hand or arm to gently push downward and backward on the front of their hip to force the adversary to fall onto their buttocks.

Timbilan Kaki Tujuh

This sweep utilizes opposing force on the upper and lower body. To begin, Step in front of the adversary's right foot with your left foot, utilizing Masukan Kaki Tujuh. Once your feet are settled, slide your left foot backwards, causing their foot to move. Simultaneously use your left hand or arm to gently push downward and forward on the back of their hip to force the adversary to fall onto their face.

Timbilan Kaki Delapan

This sweep utilizes opposing force on the upper and lower body. To begin, Step in front of the adversary's right foot with your right foot, utilizing Masukan Kaki Delapan. Once your feet are settled, slide your right foot backwards, causing their foot to move. Simultaneously use your right hand or arm to gently push downward and backward on the front of their shoulder to force the adversary to fall onto their buttocks.

Section 3: Timbilan Tangan Described

Timbilan Tangan refers to any takedown or throw that utilizes the hands as the primary energy of the Timbilan. As such, the quantity of methods that could fall under this category is quite large. Out of necessity, we will only be exploring a limited set of these. Largely these are based on Ular method of movement. Though this is a very limited set of takedowns, be sure, there are many more takedowns and throws which could be utilized in their place.

Timbilan Tangan Satu

After striking the adversary with Masukan Tangan Satu, enter with Masukan Kaki Satu. Slap the opponent squarely in the face with your right palm as you strike the kidney with your left palm, causing the head to tip backward. Continue to push until the adversary falls backward over your leg. If you choose to, you may also add extra hits, such as elbows and knees. This could be referred to as Dorong Kepala.

Timbilan Tangan Dua

After striking the adversary with Masukan Tangan Dua, enter with Masukan Kaki Dua. Once you have entered wrap your left arm around the left side of the adversary's neck. Your right hand will be on the right side of the adversary's neck. Clasp your hands, while rotating clockwise (against a right hand lead) as you kneel to the ground. Continue to hold the head as the adversary flips over you. Of course from this position there are many follow-ups available.

Timbilan Tangan Satu

Continued...

Timbilan Tangan Dua

Timbilan Tangan Tiga

After striking the adversary with Masukan Tangan Tiga, enter with Masukan Kaki Tiga. Immediately grab the head of the adversary with both hands. Pull the head backwards as you jump backwards and to the ground, smashing their head on the ground with both hands. This is referred to as Menyangan Kelapa or the Coconut Smash. Though you probably won't need to, you can also add many additional hits in the felling process and of course add follow-ups after the adversary hits the ground.

Timbilan Tangan Tiga

Timbilan Tangan Empat

After striking the adversary with Masukan Tangan Empat, place your right hand on the right side of the neck of the adversary. Hold the right hand of the adversary with your left hand. Pull the head of the adversary down and towards their right arm. Immediately straighten the adversary's right arm as you rotate it to a vertical position, perpendicular to the floor. Continue to rotate the adversary as you step away slightly causing them to fall onto their back. This is called Putar Kepala Dalam or Inside Head Turning Throw. You may wish to retain the arm for use in follow-up techniques.

Timbilan Tangan Empat

Timbilan Tangan Lima

After striking the adversary with Masukan Tangan Lima, continue to drive your hand forward and along the right side of the neck, smashing the neck or the collarbone with your forearm. Simultaneously step behind the adversary's right leg with your right leg (Masukan Kaki Satu - optional) and drive the adversary backwards. As their back begins to bend, rotate your waist to the left and place the adversary on the ground. You may wish to retain the arm for use in follow-up techniques.

Timbilan Tangan Lima

Timbilan Tangan Enam

After striking the adversary with Masukan Tangan Enam, slip your left arm under the right arm of the adversary. Reaching up to their face from behind and under their arm. Pull their head backward as you also twist their body counter clockwise. This is a type of Tarik Kepala or

Head Pull. As the adversary falls you can also add knees, etc. You may want to check the adversary's left hand with your right to prevent them from grabbing you.

Timbilan Tangan Enam

Timbilan Tangan Tujuh

After striking the adversary with Masukan Tangan Tujuh, reach your left hand up and grab the nape of the adversary's neck. Pull the adversary's head forward and down as you straighten their arm into a vertical position using your right hand. Continue to turn them until they fall. This is Putar Kepala Luar or Outside Head Turning Throw. You want to retain control of the adversary's right arm to perform follow-ups and controls.

Timbilan Tangan Tujuh

Timbilan Tangan Delapan

After striking the adversary with Masukan Tangan Delapan, reach upward with your right hand, hook the crook of the elbow with the thumb edge of your hand and pull downward as your draw your right hand near to you. Then immediately use your right hand to reach up towards the adversary's chin and push their chin to the ground. Another variation of this would be to perform a Kuncian Tukul (Hammer Lock) to a timbilan.

Timbilan Tangan Delapan

Chapter 10: Totokan
Section 1: Introduction

Totokan are essential in silat, and for that matter, most other martial arts. On some level it may be viewed as similar to the Chinese Dim Mak or Dim Hsueh, however, their or no concerns about energy principles in Pencak Silat Pertempuran.

The methods of Totokan found in Pencak Silat Pertempuran are a product of the reference system created by the various Masukan of the system. The core Totokan that are trained teach the principle of attacking the body where it will have the most effect with the least effort. Additionally, what we teach could be considered to be an introduction into some of the bodies "most available" points of vulnerability. It is not all-inclusive and other points of vulnerability exist which do have a greater and potentially more devastating impact on the adversary. Those more devastating points will be covered in the Pembasmian level of study and have been deliberately left out of the study of Totokan.

Within the context of Totokan there are different methods and different tools, which can be used, for instance, the feet, knees, elbows, hands, and fingers can be used.

Section 2: Totokan Described

The purpose of the Totokan as performed within Pencak Silat Pertempuran has already been discussed to some degree. However, it must also be understood, that Totokan do offer us an option for showing mercy where a pain compliance may be used, or a specific attack performed, that's effects while painful and potentially incapacitating, are only temporary in their effectiveness. That is to say, that after a few minutes, an adversary could and should mostly recover. Additionally, Totokan can also be used as a method of manipulating an adversary's body structure, alignment, resolve, or will to get a specific result or to show additional opportunities for techniques or controls which may be effectively used. Totokan are not to be relied on as fight ending but like many things are considered to be part of the philosophy of "Langkah dari batuan ke batuan!"

2a: Totok Tangan Described

Totok Tangan are those methods which employ the hands, arms, and elbows as the primary method for striking, pressing, and pinching vulnerable targets. These are primarily nerves, but are not limited to nerve striking. A basic list of targets not covered in the Totokan that are demonstrated include: pinching, grabbing, or squeezing the lips, cheeks, ears, carotid, trapezius muscles, brachial plexus, triceps, the side of the fingertip's, cuticle's, nipples, abdominal obliques, and inner thighs.

As with all things, Totok Tangan are based off of the Ales and Masukan Tangan. It is acceptable to use Masukan Kaki, but not necessary in most cases.

Additionally, though it is normal that these totok take place while the attacker is striking, kicking, or pushing, there is no criteria that states that they can't be used at anytime it would be appropriate, however, the effect will change appropriately.

Totok Tangan Satu

Perform Ales Satu against a low attack to the stomach. Immediately perform Jari Tombak to the eyes of the attacker.

Totok Tangan Dua

Perform Ales Dua against a low attack to the stomach. Immediately perform Celeng Taring to the bottom side of the jawbone. Use the thumb tip to press up against the nerves along the jaw ridge. This attempts to violently strike the Mandibular Nerve.

Totok Tangan Tiga

Perform Ales Tiga against a low attack to the stomach. Immediately perform Celeng Taring to the area right behind the jaw hinge and directly beneath the ear lobe. This attempts to violently strike the Facial Nerve junction.

Totok Tangan Empat

Perform Ales Empat against a low attack to the stomach. Immediately perform Pukulan Macan Tutul the front of the attackers shoulder. Attempting to strike with enough penetration to affect the Brachial Plexus.

Totok Tangan Tiga   ***Totok Tangan Empat***

Totok Tangan Lima

Perform Ales Lima against a high attack to the head. Immediately perform Pukulan Ular Sendok to the Ribs of the attacker. This attempts to strike any of the Lateral Cutaneous branches of the Thoracic nerves.

Totok Tangan Enam

Perform Ales Enam against a high attack to the head. Immediately perform Kuku Macan to the Upper Pectoral Muscle, using the thumb opposing the fingers to active the Lateral Cutaneous branches of the Thoracic Nerve.

Totok Tangan Lima   *Totok Tangan Enam*

Totok Tangan Tujuh

Perform Ales Tujuh against a high attack to the head. Immediately perform Pukulan Pamur to the Posterior surface of the hip. This attempts to strike any of the Lateral Cutaneous branches of the Iliohypogastric Nerve.

Totok Tangan Delapan

Perform Ales Delapan against a high attack to the head. Immediately perform Pukulan Sterlak to the lower abdomen of the attacker. This attempts to deeply and violently strike the bladder, pressing the bladder against the pelvic bone. This will also likely aggravate the Iliohypogastric Nerve.

Totok Tangan Tujuh   **Totok Tangan Delapan**

2b: Totok Kaki Described

Totok Kaki are those methods, which employ the use of the knees, feet, or shins as the primary method for kicking, and hitting vulnerable targets. These are primarily nerves, but are not limited to nerve striking. The use of Totok Kaki is generally pre-Ales. That is, that they occur slightly before the necessity of the Ales exists. However, they are still based primarily on the Ales and as such, the Ales dictates which foot is free, what the attack might be and what body movements you are performing generally. Additionally, these could be called Sepak Totok since they are delivered as kicks.

Additionally, though it is normal that these totok take place while the attacker is stepping, there is no criteria that states that they can't be used at anytime it would be appropriate, however, the effect will change appropriately.

On another note, Masukan Lutut could also be classified as Totok Kaki. The primary difference, as they are taught, is to bump the leg with the knee as it is placed into position. This requires the proper use of timing, while the Totok are used as a defensive tool when your timing is off. That said, a knee could deliver quite a blow to the legs of an attacker, which can actually cause the attacker to become unconscious.

Totok Kaki Satu

As the attacker steps forward to deliver an attack, you should kick forward with the ball of your foot (Similar to Sepak Sekop), impeding their forward progress, causing pain and unbalancing them. Use your right foot against a right step essentially performing Ales Satu.

Totok Kaki Satu

Totok Kaki Dua

As the attacker steps forward to deliver an attack, you should kick forward with the ball of your foot (Similar to Sepak Sekop), impeding their forward progress, causing pain and unbalancing them. Use your left foot against a right step essentially performing Ales Dua.

Totok Kaki Tiga

As the attacker steps forward to deliver an attack, you should kick forward with the heel of your foot (Use a Dapuan kick or you can also think of it as the beginning of the Sepak Naga kick since the Dapuan is just a portion of the Sepak Naga), impeding their forward progress, causing pain and unbalancing them. Use your right foot against a right step essentially performing Ales Tiga.

Totok Kaki Dua   *Totok Kaki Tiga*

Totok Kaki Empat

As the attacker steps forward to deliver an attack, you should kick forward with the heel of your foot (Use a Dapuan kick or you can also think of it as the beginning of the Sepak Naga kick since the Dapuan is just a portion of the Sepak Naga), impeding their forward progress, causing pain and unbalancing them. Use your left foot against a right step essentially performing Ales Empat.

Totok Kaki Lima

As the attacker steps forward to deliver an attack, you should kick forward with the side of your foot (use Tendangan Rusuk or Sepak Iris), impeding their forward progress, causing pain and unbalancing them. Use your right foot against a right step essentially performing Ales Lima.

Totok Kaki Empat

Totok Kaki Enam

As the attacker steps forward to deliver an attack, you should kick forward with the side of your foot (use Tendangan Rusuk or Sepak Iris), impeding their forward progress, causing pain and unbalancing them. Use your left foot against a right step essentially performing Ales Enam.

Totok Kaki Tujuh

This version is slightly different. As the attack is delivered, perform your Ales. As soon as the step is completed, deliver a Tendangan Ular Sanca kick to the Inner Thigh or knee. Use your right leg against a right step.

Totok Kaki Enam   *Totok Kaki Tujuh*

Totok Kaki Delapan

Similarly to Totok Kaki Tujuh, as the attack is delivered, perform your Ales. As soon as the step is completed, deliver a Tendangan Ular Sanca kick to the Outer Thigh or knee. Use your Left leg against a right step.

Totok Kaki Delapan

Chapter 11: Perisai
Section 1: Introduction

Perisai is the word Pencak Silat Pertempuran uses to describe movements, which are intentionally designed to act as barriers for oncoming attacks. This is a necessary component to silat or any martial art for that matter. Most martial arts would refer to these as blocks, but in our system they are a bit more fluid than a prescribed block.

The methods for Perisai in PSP are a product of the reference system created by the various Ales of the system. The core Perisai are trained to teach the principle of off-timing. That is, that they demonstrate an option for defense when your timing of movement or engagement is slightly behind the opponents. It is not the preferred method since the timing advantage is the opponents.

Within the context of Perisai there are different methods and different tools, which can be used, for instance, the feet, shins, knees, elbows, hips, shoulders, fists, hands, and forearms can be used. Not all of these are explored within the confines of the curriculum but that doesn't mean they shouldn't be explored.

Section 2: Perisai Described

The purpose of the Perisai as performed within Pencak Silat Pertempuran has already been discussed to some degree. However, it must also be understood, that Perisai do offer us an option for those times when our timing is off or slow as a method to regain the timing. In fact, Perisai may also be damaging or employ an aspect of Totokan but they are primarily designed to be a last wall of defense for self-preservation and protection. Additionally, Perisai can also be used as a method of manipulating an adversary's body structure, alignment, resolve, or will to get a specific result or to show additional opportunities for ending the conflict. Perisai are not to be relied on as fight ending but like many things are considered to be part of the philosophy of "Langkah dari batuan ke batuan!"

One major point of difference between the use of Perisai and other types of defense found in Pencak Silat Pertempuran is the use of the Perisai to stop the attack in a directly opposing manner. That is to say, that these are not parries but blocks.

Additionally, the downside to defending yourself in this manner is the lack of over extension and vulnerability these cause the attacker. For instance if I am attacked and I block the attack. The attacker is normally free to attack immediately with another attack, since my Perisai does nothing to necessarily disrupt the attackers structure. Whereas a parry, or the use of our normal Ales methodology, cause the attacker to over extend their attack and, as a result, their physical structure is disrupted which often makes it difficult for them to develop a continuous attack. However, by including in your mindset a more aggressive application to the Perisai, such as using the Perisai as an attack, you will have a greater likelihood of disrupting the attacker and further attacks.

2a: Pukulan Described

Perisai Pukulan are those methods which employ the fists and forearms primarily for the sole purpose of defending yourself against an attacker. They can of course, also be used to destroy the attackers arms or legs by using the Perisai as an attack.

Perisai Pukulan is primarily a defensive tool but when used offensively can be used to attack muscle groups or sensitive nerve areas.

Perisai Pukulan Satu
Perform Ales Satu against a low, Belakang Pukul Tukul attack to the stomach, using the forearm or fist to attack the inner portion of the wrist or the arm of the attacker in a blocking manner.

Perisai Pukulan Dua
Perform Ales Dua against a low, Pukul Sabit, Pukul Naik, or Pukul Sterlak, to the stomach, using the forearm

or fist to attack the inner portion of the wrist or arm of the attacker in a blocking manner.

Perisai Pukul Satu   **Perisai Pukul Dua**

Perisai Pukulan Tiga

Perform Ales Tiga against a low, Belakang Pukul Tukul attack to the stomach, using the forearm of one hand and the forearm of the other to attack the arm and wrist of the attacker in a blocking manner.

Perisai Pukulan Empat

Perform Ales Empat against a low, Pukul Sabit, Pukul Naik, or Pukul Sterlak, to the stomach, using the forearm of one hand and the forearm of the other to attack the arm and wrist of the attacker in a blocking manner.

Perisai Pukulan Lima

Perform Ales Lima against a high, Pukul Belakang, Pukul Pamur, or Pukul Sterlak (as examples), to the head, using the forearm or fist of one hand to attack the triceps muscle, and the palm of the other, to protect your face. The palm can also be used as a fist creating the opportunity for an inadvertent hit on the attacker's wrist.

Perisai Pukul Empat   *Perisai Pukul Lima*

Perisai Pukulan Enam

Perform Ales Enam against a high, Pukul Sabit or Pukul Pamur, to the head, using the forearm or fist of one hand to strike the bicep muscle, and the palm of the other, to protect your face. Additionally, the palm used for protection can also be held as a fist to potentially cause minor pain to the wrist of an attacker.

Perisai Pukulan Enam

Perisai Pukulan Tujuh

Perform Ales Tujuh against a high, Pukul Belakang, Pukul Pamur, or Pukul Sterlak (as examples), to the head, using the forearm or fist of one hand, striking near the shoulder and on the Triceps muscle, and the palm of the other, to attack the bicep or forearm of the attacker while protecting your face.

Perisai Pukulan Delapan

Perform Ales Delapan against a high, Pukul Sabit, Pukul Pamur, or even a Papisau (as examples), to the head, using the palm of the hand furthest away and the fist of the hand closest to the shoulder of the attacking hand. Strike the bicep muscle with the fist, near the shoulder, or strike the brachial plexus nerve at the front of the shoulder. Additionally, you may also use your palm as a fist to attack the wrist or forearm of the attacking hand.

Perisai Pukulan Tujuh   **Perisai Pukulan Delapan**

2b: Siku Described

Pukulan Siku are those methods which employ the elbows primarily and to some extent the forearms for the sole purpose of defending yourself against an attacker. They can of course, also be used to destroy the attackers arms or legs by using the Perisai as an attack.

Pukulan Siku is primarily a defensive tool but when used offensively can be used to attack muscle groups or sensitive nerve areas and to some extent the joints of an attacker.

Perisai Siku Satu

Perform Ales Satu against a low, Belakang Pukul Tukul attack to the stomach, using the elbow to defend the kidney and side by using Siku Belakang to attack the inner or outer portion of the wrist or the arm of the attacker in a blocking manner.

Perisai Siku Dua

Perform Ales Dua against a low, Pukul Sabit, Pukul Naik, or Pukul Sterlak, to the stomach, using the elbow to defend the kidney and side by using Siku Belakang to attack the inner portion of the wrist or the arm of the attacker in a blocking manner.

Perisai Siku Satu   *Perisai Siku Dua*

Perisai Siku Tiga

Perform Ales Tiga against a low, Belakang Pukul Tukul attack to the stomach. Use the Siku Jatuh of one arm to block the elbow, triceps, or forearm, and the forearm of the other to attack the arm or wrist of the attacker in a blocking manner.

Perisai Siku Empat

Perform Ales Empat against a low, Pukul Sabit, Pukul Naik, or Pukul Sterlak, to the stomach. Use the Siku Jatuh of one arm to block the bicep or forearm, and the forearm of the other to attack the arm or wrist of the attacker in a blocking manner.

Perisai Siku Tiga   *Perisai Siku Empat*

Perisai Siku Lima

Perform Ales Lima against a high, Pukul Belakang, Pukul Pamur, or Pukul Sterlak (as examples), to the head. Use the elbow in a Siku Belakang diagonally upward to attack the elbow, forearm, or wrist of the attacker.

Perisai Siku Enam

Perform Ales Enam against a high, Pukul Sabit or Pukul Pamur, to the head. Use the elbow in a Siku Belakang diagonally upward to attack the biceps, forearm, or inner wrist of the attacker.

Perisai Siku Lima   *Perisai Siku Enam*

Perisai Siku Tujuh

Perform Ales Tujuh against a high, Pukul Belakang, Pukul Pamur, or Pukul Sterlak (as examples), to the head. Use Siku Jatuh to defend the attack by striking the triceps, elbow, or forearm of the attacker. Use your secondary hand to protect the face.

Perisai Siku Delapan

Perform Ales Tujuh against a high, Pukul Belakang, Pukul Pamur, or Pukul Sterlak (as examples), to the head. Use Siku Jatuh to defend the attack by striking the Biceps, bottom of the elbow, or forearm of the attacker. Use your secondary hand to protect the face from the potential follow through of the attackers hand.

Perisai Siku Tujuh   **Perisai Siku Delapan**

Chapter 12: Seni
Section 1: Introduction

You may have heard it said that Pencak Silat is both Seni and Beladiri. That is, that it is both art and self-defense. In fact, most would say that Pencak means art and silat means combat. Putting them together then means something akin to martial art or combat art, etcetera; however, Indonesian guru-guru are still disputing the meanings of these words. In large part, this is due to the variance of regional dialects and languages.

Before we are too sidetracked however, the purpose of this section is to discuss the relationship between the martial and the artistic - not the linguistic issues of Indonesia.

Often when discussed, Seni and Beladiri are treated as two distinct items, one being purely aesthetic and the other being purely concerned with battle skills, though the two, are rarely separable.

Speaking from personal experiences it has often been the case that martial artists break themselves into two categories: Traditionalists and Modernists. The Traditionalists can largely be described for the sake of argument as those who embrace fully all aspects of the martial arts: Combat, Spiritual, Sport or Aesthetic, and Cultural. Modernists on the other hand are typically seen as those who are mostly concerned with Combat and or

Sport and want to do away with the Spiritual, Cultural, and even the Aesthetic on some level.

Wherever you fall generally in the two main categories there will no doubt be variance to what degree you might consider yourself a Traditionalist or Modernist or even agree with my two categories at all. It won't affect what the point of this section is in either case.

With the groundwork laid, let's move on to the foundation question. Is the artistic aspect of the martial arts and more specifically Pencak Silat detrimental to combat? More specifically, can the artistic aspects of Pencak Silat be USEFUL to my combat skills?

Having gone back and forth with this issue for years even before I was involved with Pencak Silat, I have decided that the answer is yes. To explain: Seni and Beladiri cannot be fully separated AND to try WILL reduce the combat effectiveness of your Pencak Silat. However, I will also say that it appears that removing certain things, depending on the system, may not interfere at all with the combat effectiveness of the system. That is not the case in our own system. Everything that is taught in Pencak Silat Pertempuran has either a direct application in combat or a developmental application to combat. Additionally, we do not view the artistic as strictly artistic, nor do we view all that is considered to be combative as being for combat. The reality is, that much of what is taught in silat and other martial arts is considered to be combat directed or applicable and yet many are the martial artists, including myself, who have found that when the "rubber meets the road," our skills are lacking somehow. Yet, while in the training hall, we have great technical mastery of the skills we have trained. How is this possible? Why is it that our combat training doesn't always allow us to utilize all of the tools we have been "developing?" The traditionalist will say that it's because we haven't trained long enough. On the other hand, the MMA types think it's because what we are training is not practical. Both extremes are wrong. In reality, there are few real martial arts masters in existence who have trained exclusively in one martial art, doing one methodology of training, that have obtained success. This is why so many of the people who have skill have gone on to study multiple arts. Additionally, the MMA types out there have given up on all that is not developed quickly and does not suit them immediately. The reality is that the MMA types will eventually have to go back to gain deeper skills – they just don't know it yet.

So, why does this gap between reality and training take place? Largely it happens for one of two reasons. A system places too much emphasis on skill development or too much emphasis on combat development. Either situation will lead to a hole in your skills and ultimate development. In reality, their needs to be a focused approach to both, this will lead to the ultimate development of your attributes. Attribute development is both combat and skill development.

That said, within the martial art of pencak silat generally, there is at least the possibility of attribute development built into it. That is not to say that somehow silat is superior, since development of attributes is somewhat individualistic. Therefore, it is difficult if not impossible for one system to obtain the perfect plan for everyone, however, silat does have within it, tools that are already purposed for that development and will meet the pesilat halfway. That is to say, that the pesilat is also responsible and must make a concerted effort to continue to explore the development of the necessary attributes.

Often referred to as bunga, the flower of silat, it contains many other components that appear to be primarily artistic in nature. Some of these are clapping, slapping the body, sikap pasang, gerakan, and even those of Langkah to minor extent. These components of seni are at least a large portion of what makes it Pencak Silat.

Section 2: Sikap Pasang

In Pencak Silat Pertempuran one of the foundational components of Seni are the Sikap Pasang. These positions are not stances, per se, but by their nature do contain stances. Rather, these are postures that are extracted from within the various jurus-jurus and other components that make up the system.

The Sikap Pasang do not work independently, rather, we also utilize various Gerakan to teach us how to move between the Sikap Pasang. The Sikap Pasang postures are designed to "invite" a predictable attack to a specific part of your body so that you can more readily respond with an appropriate defense or counter attack. Additionally, the Sikap Pasang also keeps us in a state of readiness without the appearance of a guard type position.

With that basic premise understood you must make the opening "welcoming." You cannot expect someone to attack you if they feel that you aren't open or you are leading them into a trap. It is a fine line between enough exposure and over-exposure, much of which has to do with range and your own personal abilities.

The postures of Sikap Pasang are innumerable. In fact, the entirety of jurus-jurus can be performed as Sikap Pasang only. That said, Sikap Pasang are not fixed postures, but postures that are found within what you already do.

Section 3: Demonstrated

The photos that follow the names of the Sikap Pasang do a good job of illustrating the position quite well, so no further explanation will be given.

Sikap Pasang Satu and Dua:

Sikap Pasang Tiga and Empat:

Sikap Pasang Lima and Enam:

Sikap Pasang Tujuh and Delapan:

Examples of other Sikap Pasang:

Section 4: Gerakan

The Gerakan of Pencak Silat Pertempuran (Combat Silat) are used in concert with Sikap Pasang and Langkah for moving from "point A to point B" without offering apparent openings or openings that are intentional and constantly changing.

In initial training the Gerakan are predetermined for the pesilat. This is primarily just a method to teach a pesilat how to move in a basic and simplistic way in personal combat. Ultimately, however, the pesilat creates their own gerakan once they understand it. It is primarily a method for moving around, and or stalking an attacker that is personal and expressive. As in Sikap Pasang, much of what you already do in Pencak Silat Pertempuran can be thought of and displayed as Gerakan. This might include Ales, Masukan, and parts of jurus-jurus, etc. As well, there are specific elements which can be added such as Four Corner Slapping and clapping the hands together as well.

Gerakan are normally used in conjunction with Sikap Pasang and Langkah to formulate a comfortable movement pattern for yourself that at one moment shows vulnerability and at another allows you to manipulate the angles and positions to gain the advantage. Additionally, the combination of these two components, gerakan and sikap pasang, can also be used as a method to distract an opponent before attacking.

4a: Gerakan Demonstrated

When performing the Gerakan it is not necessary to use the Ales themselves since these are neither offensive nor defensive necessarily, though the Gerak, if explored, can be both offensive and defensive. Also, the Gerak can and should be added together with Langkah to create the full movement. It is not necessary to define the Langkah specifically since all Langkah should be explored. Additionally, the Gerakan shown in the following photos are merely a portion of what is possible since this is a discussion of movement. As a result, photos cannot do justice to the actual movements themselves. Use these movements only as a basic foundation for developing your own movements.

Gerakan Satu and Dua

Utilize your hands similarly to Ales Satu and Dua. In the instance shown in the photos, the left hand is nearest and the right hand is furthest away. Additionally both hands will sweep across the body to the right side in this instance. Your lead hand may either use the back palm or the palm itself to "push" to the side. As well, you may use both the back palm and the palm by adding a small circle of the hand.

These can be done leading with the back palm movement or the palm movement and then moving to the movement that has not yet been completed.

The energy of these Gerak-gerak is one of brushing aside when using the backhand and one of a downward forward corkscrew when using the palm.

The photos depict Gerak Satu. To perform Gerak Dua simply mirror the photos and instructions provided.

Using the back palm...

Using the palm.

Gerakan Tiga and Empat

Utilize your hands similarly to Masukan Tangan Tiga and Empat. In the first photo, the left hand is nearest and the right hand is furthest away. Additionally both hands will sweep across the body from the right side to the left, exchanging positions from top to bottom, in order to perform Gerakan Empat.

The energy of these Gerak-gerak is one of hacking.

The photos depict Gerakan Tiga on the left and Gerakan Empat on the right with the transition photo in between.

Gerakan Lima and Enam

Utilize your hands similarly to Masukan Tangan Lima and Enam. In the first photo, the right hand is nearest and the left hand is furthest away.

Your Left hand will perform a parry type of action near the shoulder while your right hand will perform a spiraling motion that starts with your palm down and rotates until the palm is facing upward. The initial motion of the right arm is quite large but as the rotation takes place the motion focuses more on the hand itself.

The energy of these Gerak-gerak is one of a forward corkscrew.

The photos depict Gerakan Lima. To perform Gerakan Enam mirror these directions.

Gerakan Tujuh and Delapan

The movements of the hands are slightly different in this Gerakan as a way of showing the possibilities that exist. The end positioning of the Gerakan is similar to that of the Masukan Tangan.

For Gerakan Tujuh, your Right hand will perform a counter-clockwise circle at shoulder height, turning until the palm is facing obliquely upward and outward from the body. Additionally, the Left hand, which is furthest away, will simply rise up to shoulder height, palm upward with the arm mostly extended.

The energy of these Gerak-gerak is one of lifting and drawing or pulling something to you.

The photos depict Gerakan Tujuh. To perform Gerakan Delapan mirror these directions.

Section 5: Bunga Introduced

The term Bunga is not always used. Many silat systems use the variant term Kembangan. Essentially the two are the same, however, there may be large differences in how bunga is performed from one aliran to the next. In my own experience I have found that often systems from Java and surrounding areas use the term Kembangan while systems related more to Sumatra use the term Bunga.

In any case, I think you will agree that the very word itself is one that does not speak directly to combat. As such, it is easy to mistake something termed as a flower for being of little or no use in combat. However, while it is true that some forms of Bunga appear to hold little or no direct value in actual combat, it has great value in preparation and training for combat. It can be said that it is the flower that leads to the fruit of silat. Bunga is a means by which a pesilat can develop characteristics of grace, fluidity of movement, timing, rhythm, and ultimately adaptability in technique.

The expressions of bunga in silat are varied. Many systems only use formalized bunga or kembangan. Some systems utilize a form-like recitation of style specific movements (Gerakan), Pukulan, Sepak, Langkah, or postures (sikap) performed with the aid of a musical orchestra and having a specific musical pattern that the pesilat will adhere to when performing. However, some systems, such as Pamur, do not use "fixed" kembangan (or an orchestra) but rather free-style kembangan, that is, they will mix and match components of their system together at random to "create" kembangan.

Additionally, some aliran perform bunga solo while others perform it with an "opponent" or training partner. For those that perform with a training partner, there are again, a few variations. For instance, some aliran use a method of practice where one pesilat imitates the others, while other aliran use a freestyle method where no mimicking is utilized and the pesilat each perform their own respective expression of bunga. Still others use both methods, as do we.

Bunga Tunas is the most basic form of Bunga within Pencak Silat Pertempuran. It is performed through a process of emulation and requires that the novice train with someone of greater skill in movement.

During this level of training it is the sole responsibility of the anak buah to emulate the abang or guru. That is, that the pesilat should mimic the movements and postures of the abang while in motion, as if looking in a mirror. The point of this level of bunga training is to build confidence of movement, balance, fluidity, and timing.

5b: Bunga Kembang

Bunga Kembang is the second level of Bunga within Pencak Silat Pertempuran. On this level, the pesilat begins to move in a personal way, expressing a personal movement style. They no longer emulate the guru or abang. Instead, they begin mixing into the movement their own movements and characteristics. This is performed solo just for personal development but should be thought of as a type of meditation where the pesilat thinks of an attacker as they practice. In Bunga Kembang the pesilat is practicing primarily to become comfortable with movements from the jurus-jurus, gerakan, sikap pasang, and langkah.

Bunga Mekar is the third and final level of Bunga within Pencak Silat Pertempuran. On this level, as the pesilat performs this bunga it should be berpasangan. This bunga is a form of distance sparring. Basically, during this process, two pesilat oppose each other and perform Bunga as though countering each other's attacks. However, at this stage, contact is not made and it is predominately used to develop timing, awareness, stamina, fluidity, confidence, and an understanding of distance.

On another note, at higher levels of Bunga Mekar it is possible to use your expression to trick an opponent by showing them "apparent" flaws or weaknesses in your skills or defenses.

Section 6: Final Thoughts

Bunga in its various forms could be thought of as a progression for developing combat abilities. For instance, a pesilat could begin their study of bunga by performing a formalized bunga – solo. That is, a pattern that is predetermined and defined by the guru. This could help to develop fluidity of movement and grace. Later, once the pesilat was able to do this well, they could perform a formalized bunga with a partner, performing the same movements, at the same time. This could help to continue the development of all previous attributes AND add the attribute of timing to the training as well as observation or recognition. This could eventually lead to freestyle bunga - solo and ultimately freestyle bunga berpasangan (with a partner). Working freestyle with a partner would develop your sense of timing, distance, recognition, fluidity of movement, and grace.

Taking that a step further, the bunga can be taken into the realm of direct application. The first step of this transition would be a counter to a single attack. The second step would be to allow the pesilat to counter the initial counter, and so on until we move into the realm of sparring. This of course develops all combat related attributes including adaptability. This is called "main" or permainan silat meaning "to play silat". This can be trained slowly at first with progressively faster and more controlled counters until; to the untrained person it may appear as a choreographed dance (until someone clearly loses - that is). Of course the pesilat know that this dance is not choreographed at all...

Section 7: Finer Points of Seni

Seni is a necessary component to my silat and yours. Eventually, if you have any doubts, you will realize that seni is only seni when it is viewed as seni since many of the movements involved in seni are directly applicable to combat. The movements of seni may not be the actual strikes or kicks, but many of the hand movements within seni can be used to distract, direct the attention or focus, and orchestrate attacks. Additionally, the eyes can be used to distract, "hypnotize," and direct attacks too. As well, the use of the feet is varied and can, when used delicately, be useful in directing attention, distracting, and luring an opponent as well as keeping your options open for Langkah.

However, this view of seni "versus" combat is not the complete story. It is merely the 10,000 ft. view of seni silat. In many ways this is what makes pencak silat such a deep and meaningful art. "For without the flower there is no fruit." It's not an accidental analogy.

To be honest, the justification as to whether or not seni is useful in combat is irrelevant because it assumes that if seni is not, that it is not useful. That simply is not true. Seni as art only is generally believed to be about grace, beauty, expression, and creativity. It is the antithesis of war or combat to most, and as such is useful as a method of balancing the study of combat mentally as well as physically.

Chapter 13: Langkah
Section 1: Introduction

To be sure, a whole book could and should be devoted just to the study and development of Langkah. Langkah are the stepping methods used by the lower body when there is need to stalk an opponent, cover long distances, move from one opponent to another, or even simply to change the angle of attack or defense. Within the context of one-on-one close quarters combat, Masukan Kaki are considered the primary stepping methods of Pencak Silat Pertempuran (Combat Silat), however, the Masukan are derivative steps drawn from the Langkah which in and of themselves do not hold all of the answers, thus the need for learning complete Langkah.

Langkah come in many different forms and styles. There are many commonly known names for Langkah but rarely are they performed identically from one Aliran to the next. Some of the more commonly known Langkah are: Langkah Satu, Langkah Dua, Langkah Tiga, Langkah Empat, Langkah Lima and Langkah Sembilan. For these there are also different names such as Langkah Jalan and Langkah Garis, which are similar, if not identical to Langkah Satu. However, it is not quite that easy since many of these Langkah have more than a few variations. For instance Langkah Garis contains both Luar and Dalam stepping methods. This can also be seen of Langkah Empat. As well, Langkah Lima is sometimes performed as a cross and sometimes as an X, similarly to what is done in the Kali male and female triangles.

The designation of the number behind the term Langkah is normally indicative of the quantity of steps involved in the Langkah, though it also generally refers to the shape of the stepping pattern. For instance, Langkah Tiga is used generally to refer to a triangle stepping pattern. This can have three steps to a side (Langkah Tiga Luar) or be small and have one step to each side (Langkah Tiga Dalam or just Langkah Tiga). Langkah Dua is often done in the shape of a U and is normally comprised of 2 steps, one for each vertical portion of the U shape. Langkah Dua as performed in PSP does differ slightly from the standard U shape. Langkah Empat is normally a square, however the square can be comprised of four steps to a side (Langkah Empat Luar) or four total steps (Langkah Empat Dalam or just Langkah Empat).

At any rate, within Pencak Silat Pertempuran (Combat Silat) there are a number of different Langkah utilized. Each is a foundation piece to the next. However, in reality there are only two Langkah in Pencak Silat Pertempuran just as there are only two Masukan Kaki. The rest are simply continuations or extrapolations of these two. The two primary Langkah are Langkah Garis Dalam and Langkah Garis Luar. From these two the rest of the Langkah can be found.

Section 2: Langkah Explained

Ultimately, Langkah are just a tool like so many other things. They will take you far in understanding if you devote yourself to the study AND application of them but they are only as useful as the person is who practices them.

Within Pencak Silat Pertempuran we utilize many different Langkah, Not all of which will be addressed in this book. For instance: Langkah Garis Dalam, Langkah Garis Luar, Langkah Dua, Langkah Tiga, Langkah Empat Dalam, Langkah Empat Luar, Langkah Lima Salib, Langkah Lima Diagonal, Langkah Harimau of various types, as well as Langkah drills such as Langkah Bintang Berpasangan and Kaki Lengket.

When stepping forward with the Langkah try to control your step length so that you are able to remain back-weighted. This is called light stepping or Pijak Baru.

Section 3: Langkah Garis

The primary stepping method from which most other methods are drawn from makes this Langkah very important. Though it is somewhat simplistic, it is the simplicity that holds the value.

Langkah Garis Dalam is stepping with your toes facing inward. That is, if your hips and shoulders are inline, your feet will also be. Sometimes this is referred to as a "Bladed Foot Position."

Step forward until your leg is extended and set your heel down on the ground. Do not shift forward until your heel is resting on the ground. Then simply shift your weight forward, letting your toe and hips turn inward and face in the same direction as your shoulders.

There is no need to slide the toe of the foot on the ground prior to setting down your heel.

Langkah Garis Luar is stepping with your toes facing outward. That is, that your hips and shoulders are inline, one foot will also be. Sometimes this is referred to as a "Cross Step."

Step forward until your leg is extended and set your heel down on the ground. Do not shift forward until your heel is resting on the ground. Then as you shift your weight forward, turn your foot outward and let the rear foot adjust as necessary. This is predominately a single weighted step, meaning that only one leg will hold the weight of the whole body.

There is no need to slide the toe of the foot on the ground prior to setting down your heel and it is not necessary to have the rear foot completely flat on the ground.

Section 4: Langkah Dua

The secondary stepping method from which all other methods are drawn from also makes this Langkah important. Though it is somewhat simplistic in nature it is a building block for other Langkah. Langkah Dua can contain elements of the Ales and Ales Tangan as well. Sometimes Langkah Dua is performed as a U shaped stepping pattern, as in Sterlak Silat.

4a: Langkah Dua

Langkah Dua is basically a stepping pattern that is formulated around a line shape. The primary purpose is to teach side-to-side stepping in conjunction with Pijak Baru or light stepping. Additionally, it is the precursor to the Langkah Tiga, Empat, and Lima.

Basic Langkah Dua

Variations using ales

Section 5: Langkah Tiga

Langkah Tiga is probably one of the most well known Langkah in existence here in the U.S. It is the primary Langkah of many of the Aliran here in the U.S. as well as abroad. Langkah Tiga is normally performed on a triangle comprising of either three steps to a side or a single step to a side. In the aliran I have been exposed to, the Langkah Tiga is the primary method for training the Sapuan and Dapuan. Sometimes the terminology is different, such as Sapu and Beset, but the basic principle is the same. The Langkah Tiga is used as a method for training sweeping, tripping, takedowns, and 360 degree combat awareness.

As I mentioned previously, Langkah Tiga can be performed as both Luar and Dalam. In Perguruan PSP we perform Langkah Tiga Dalam, that is to say, that we only perform "one step" to each side of the triangle versus three steps to each side of the triangle.

Langkah Tiga is often thought of as being a largely Javanese influenced methodology of movement.

5a: Langkah Tiga

To perform Langkah Tiga, imagine or draw a triangle on the ground. The triangle should be an equilateral triangle, meaning all sides should be the same length. (The sides should be slightly longer than your average step length.)

To begin, stand on the lower right corner of the triangle base with both feet. Step to the left with your left foot to the opposite corner of the triangle base facing the center of the triangle. Immediately slide your right foot to your left performing a Dapuan.

Continue by turning in a counterclockwise circle, so your back is facing the point of the triangle and you are looking out away from the triangle. Slide your left foot backwards along the line of the triangle to its point.

Turn your body so you are now looking at the center of the triangle and slide your right foot to the point of the triangle. Immediately pivot on your left foot, turning counterclockwise.

Set your right foot down and perform a left Sapuan. Rotate your body counterclockwise and slide your right foot along the line of the triangle performing a Dapuan.

Langah Tiga continued

At this point you have arrived at your starting point and may either continue or stop.

Also you may add hand movements to represent pushing, pressing, pulling, and bracing to help you visualize your practice of Langkah Tiga.

When performing the Langkah Tiga, you may rotate at the corners in either a counterclockwise or clockwise motion and should do both for a more complete understanding. Additionally, Langkah Tiga (dalam) largely represents not only the aspect of sweeping, tripping, etc. but also the overall component of entering which is required to perform the other aspects.

Section 6: Langkah Empat

It doesn't seem that Langkah Empat is as prominent here in the U.S. as Langkah Tiga and largely that could be because much of the silat here in the U.S. is influenced by Javanese silat and Langkah Empat is more of an influence of Sumatran Silat it seems.

As I mentioned previously, Langkah Empat can be performed as both Luar and Dalam. In Perguruan PSP we perform both, however, our Langkah Empat Luar and Langkah Empat Dalam are similar and do not comprise taking four steps to one side of the square for Langkah Empat Luar. Instead, the primary difference between Langkah Empat Luar and Langkah Empat Dalam is the method of "turning the corner." Langkah Empat Luar moves you further from the opponent and Langkah Empat Dalam moves you closer as you turn the corner of the square.

Langkah Empat is a langkah, which teaches you to move around an attacker.

To start Langkah Empat Dalam, stand on the lower right corner of the square. Step out with your left foot as though performing Ales Lima.

Slide your right foot to your left and touch your toe. Step forward on the line with your right foot to the corner.

Bring your left foot to your right and turn counterclockwise on the point of the corner so that you are turning towards the square. Touch your left foot on the ground and then continue to step on to the next corner with your left foot.

Bring your right foot to your left and touch your toe down. Step forward on the line with your right foot to the corner. Bring your left foot to your right and turn counterclockwise on the point of the corner so that you are turning towards the square. You should now be at the starting point.

continued...

Empat Dalam continued

6b: Langkah Empat Luar

To start Langkah Empat Dalam, stand on the lower right corner of the square. Step out with your left foot as though performing Ales Lima.

Slide your right foot to your left and touch your toe. Step forward on the line with your right foot to the corner but turn your toe outward as in Depok or Langkah Garis Luar.

Make a circular step with your left foot and turn clockwise on the point of the corner so that you are turning away from the square. Continue to step on to the next corner with your left foot without pausing. You should now be facing the square again.

Bring your right foot to your left and touch your toe down. Step forward on the line with your right foot to the corner.

Make a circular step with your left foot and turn clockwise on the point of the corner so that you are turning away from the square. Continue to step on to the next corner with your left foot without pausing. You should now be facing the square again and at the starting point. You may also simply rotate and put your fee together on the corner to complete the training.

Completing the training.

Section 7: Langkah Lima

Langkah Lima is the culmination of Langkah Garis, Langkah Dua, Langkah Tiga, and Langkah Empat. It is a very versatile Langkah and is used as a method for dealing with multiple attackers. You may use any of the kuda-kuda, sikap pasang, gerakan, sempok, or depok.

As I mentioned previously, Langkah Lima can be performed as both Salib and also as an X.

7a: Langkah Lima Salib

Langkah Lima Salib is a cross. The term Salib means crucifix.

To begin Langkah Lima Salib you must either draw or imagine a cross on the ground. Step forward with your left (or right) foot, to the center of the cross. Do not move the center foot while you perform the training and application of this langkah. (You may switch whatever foot is in the center of the cross at anytime but you must always have a foot in the center of the cross.) From here you may step in any of the four directions as shown in the following photos.

Langkah Lima Salib

Langkah Lima X is in the shape of an X and is similar to both the Male and Female Triangles of Kali. (The "X" is not an official term and neither is "Salib" but they help us to communicate which version of Langkah Lima we are talking about.)

To begin Langkah Lima X you must either draw or imagine an X on the ground. Step forward with your left (or right) foot, to the center of the X. Do not move the center foot while you perform the training and application of this langkah. (You may switch whatever foot is in the center of the X at anytime but you must always have a foot in the center of the X.) From here you may step in any of the four directions as shown in the following photos.

Langkah Lima X

Section 8: Langkah Final Thoughts

When performing langkah it is also possible and expected to add all of your Huruf practice as well. In addition, you may also add the practice of the jurus–jurus components into the langkah. That said there is much more to langkah than a single pass through in a book can accomplish.

Chapter 14: Jurus jurus
Section 1: Introduction

The scope of this subject is too large for this book. As a result this topic will be covered only briefly and primarily to give the practitioner of PSP and those interested in PSP, an idea of what jurus-jurus are purposed for.

Jurus-jurus are a means in which the practitioner can learn about principles of movement. That is to say that the jurus-jurus contain movements, which are specific to a system of silat and teach the required movements of that system of silat.

Further, jurus-jurus also contain within the movements, applications, sometimes referred to as Buah, meaning fruit. These are general applications or techniques, which can be derived from the jurus-jurus and further, developed or created. In addition, Buah are not necessarily prescribed applications, rather, they are applications or techniques that can be drawn from the jurus-jurus movements and adapted to situations or drawn out for specific situations as needed. For example, a person may have a question regarding a specific attack and an appropriate defense or counter to that attack. The person would then look at the jurus-jurus of the system to find an appropriate answer from the movements contained within the various jurus-jurus of a system, similar to the idea of an Encyclopedia where movements are the various subjects or principles and can be put together to formulate a complete answer to the question. Another way to look at Buah is as an A-Z approach to the jurus where the beginning of a jurus is the beginning of the application and goes from one end of the jurus to the other in a long string.

Essentially, jurus-jurus incorporate Sambut Pukul, Tangkapan, Kuncian, Timbalan, Totokan and Pembasmian within their movements and it is up to the pesilat to extract these meanings through the addition of Langkah and Masukan Kaki.

If you view the jurus-jurus as being a pre-set, pre-arranged pattern of fighting or techniques only, you will only get one small portion of the value that is contained within them.

There are many different types of jurus-jurus and methods of utilization that various aliran silat use. The types of jurus-jurus can essentially be broken down into two primary categories consisting of Jurus-jurus Tangan and Jurus-jurus Senjata. Some aliran silat only have one set of jurus-jurus that are used for both, and meaning for a particular weapon is extrapolated. Pencak Silat Pertempuran utilizes this method for primary weapons, though secondary weapons such as Tongkat could be studied utilizing additional jurus-jurus from the various aliran silat that comprise Pencak Silat Pertempuran.

Section 2: Jurus-jurus Practice

Jurus-jurus are best studied, utilizing Rasa and visualization practices. That is, that while practicing; you put your full intention into the movements and attention to the possible Buah each movement can have. It is also a good idea to practice your jurus-jurus in different ways. As an example, you might try combining different stepping methods with your jurus-jurus as an act of exploration. Additionally, you might also include various components of the jurus-jurus together to create "spontaneous" jurus-jurus as a type of Bunga.

Chapter 15: Etcetera
Section 1: Introduction to Numbering

Of all the aspects to Combat Silat this has proven to be the most difficult aspect for people to learn and get comfortable with. It normally takes several times of showing someone this concept and repeatedly explaining why it is used before it is understood.

The point of the numbering method is not to confuse, but to instill a few very important principles into your training and develop within you a strong skill set that is more adaptable.

As I mentioned earlier in this manual, Combat Silat is founded on the idea that there are only a limited number of positions to be in, while dealing with an aggressor. To more clearly illustrate this primary principle, it is necessary to define those positions somehow and numbering them is the easiest. Using numbers specifically clearly shows how few positions there are and more quickly helps a person to recognize their position in relationship to an aggressor. This is essential when considering Combat Silat as a "GPS" system for combat or CPS (Combat Positioning System).

The numbering system is based on mirroring in relationship to your adversary. For example if your adversary strikes with their right hand, turning to the left does Ales Satu. However, if they strike with their left hand, turning to the right does Ales Satu. Likewise, if they punch with their right, turning to the right does Ales Dua and if they punch with the left, turning to the left does Ales Dua. The same type of mirroring is done throughout the entire system no matter what the technique to be applied is.

The reason for this type of mirroring is so that you will always understand that in a given position certain things can be performed. You will never think to yourself that you are doing a two when in fact you are doing a one. It also helps to define the possibilities for techniques as well as the potential outcomes.

Section 2: Introduction to Latihan Berpasangan

Latihan simply means training or exercise. All of Combat Silat is composed of Latihan in the literal sense of the word, as such, the term Latihan Berpasangan has been used to help delineate those drills that absolutely need to have the participation of another person.

Latihan Berpasangan are essentially training drills. They are designed to expose the student of Combat Silat to essential elements of fighting without exposing them to the danger of uncontrolled chaos. This allows the student to begin to understand the value of a given method or technique without fear of being seriously injured.

As a student becomes more comfortable with a drill, the intensity of the drill can usually be increased almost to the point of chaos. No drill can fully take you into chaos because it would no longer be a drill. Additionally, at the point that something becomes chaotic it no longer trains but causes us to rely on self-preservation instincts.

The primary drill to train is the Tangan Bertenun or the Weaving Hands drill. It should be worked indefinately adding and taking away elements and eventually introducing weapons into the fray. Each new element added will change the drill. The elements, which can be added, are pretty limitless and can include a majority of the curriculum that we train. For instance, you might add Ales, Masukan, Tangkapan, Kuncian, Timbilan, Totokan, Pembasmian, Senjata, and even Harimau. As well, even other Latihan Berpasangan pieces can be added to the drill.

Though I have placed an emphasis on the Tangan Bertenun Latihan Berpasangan, all of the other drills should be trained as well, for there is no drill in Combat Silat that is not essential to your development. If there were, I simply would have taken it out!

Section 3: Introduction to Pembasmian

Pembasmian are methods of combat that are hardcore destructive. If applied correctly they will result in the death or severe injury of an attacker. They are only meant for the direst of situations when the only other alternative is your own death or the death of someone else.

The methods of Pembasmian found in Pencak Silat Pertempuran are a product of the reference system created by the various Ales and Masukan and include methods of breaking, dislocating, and strangling.

Section 4: Introduction to Harimau

Harimau as it is taught in Pencak Silat Pertempuran is a combination of various animal methods that deal with groundfighting. Primarily it is comprised of Harimau, Macan, and Monyet Silat. However, various other animal elements such as crocodile (Buaya) and turtle (kura-kura) may also be found within the primary core of Harimau, Macan, and Monyet Silat. For simplicity sake, it is all referred to as Harimau and no distinction is made concerning them since from a practical perspective the methods are similar and related.

Within Pencak Silat Pertempuran (Combat Silat) the Harimau is considered a sub-system, meaning that it contains many of the same categories as the "standing" version of Pencak Silat Pertempuran. In essence, it can be considered as simply the rendah version of Combat Silat.

Harimau is a complete sub-system of Pencak Silat Pertempuran offering anyone the ability to perform street effective combat from the ground; however, it does not contain the volume of unique material found in the Tinggi version of Combat Silat. As such, once the core Tinggi system of Combat Silat is learned, the Harimau is normally viewed as a natural extension.

Section 5: Introduction to Senjata

Senjata is essentially the weapons component of Pencak Silat Pertempuran (Combat Silat). Though we contain and use traditional weapons and firearms, we also stress the ability to defend against various weapons unarmed.

Additionally, understanding of firearms to include, pistol, revolver, shotguns and any other type of firearm you can find is essential and we expect all high level Combat Silat practitioners to have ample understanding of firearms to include, safety, tactical considerations, legal considerations, and psychological considerations of use.

Pencak Silat Pertempuran also practices the use of several traditional weapons to include, Tongkat, Clurit, Pisau, Golok, Kerambit, Ikat, and Sarong.

Section 6: Introduction to Beladiri

The purpose of Bela Diri within Pencak Silat Pertempuran is to introduce scenario based ideas of personal defense as it might occur on the street and to learn to deal with new and difficult situations. In reality, there are often so many possibilities for variations that it becomes difficult to define the specific issue of self-defense.

Chapter 16: The Need For Training
Section 1: Necessity for Training

Training is primary in any endeavor. You don't run a marathon without first having trained. You don't get a 4.0 without studying. It takes effort to rise above the average player. To that end, one must look at all of life as training.

No matter who you are; how you fight; or even how you train; all combat success and success in life is 100% training. In fighting, this includes military personnel as well as civilian, knife fighting and empty hand; even for a sniper ability equals training.

There are really six different areas of training in Combat Silat. However, the six different types of training are actually only a part of three different families of training. The six areas and the three families are listed as:

Muscular and Skeletal Training

Mental and Reflexive Training

Spiritual and Moral Training

Within these six areas and three families, all martial training can be included or found. They are not system dependent. They can be found in all martial arts to a greater or lesser extent. The only determining factor is the emphasis of the art or teacher and its practitioners.

Section 2: Muscular and Skeletal Training

To explain further, Muscular Training refers to the areas of strength, elasticity, speed, agility, balance and stamina while Skeletal Training refers to the density of the bones, structural alignment, and proper care of the joints. As you can imagine these are important to all martial artists. Without physical training of any kind, the equally skilled fighter would find himself (or herself) at a disadvantage quickly. By increasing your level of physical training, you can greatly increase the probability of success in combat.

Section 3: Mental and Reflexive Training

Mental and Reflexive Training, as we are referring to it, is the relationship between action and reaction. As martial artists the training of the mind is always in direct relation to our level of physical ability. This is in large part, due to the relationship of fear with our level of ability. As our skills increase or as we continue to face our fears time and time again successfully, our fear or anxiety will lessen. You cannot eliminate fear, but you can, if given enough time, learn to cope with it, much the same as riding on a roller coaster. It always scares you, yet the fear that is created is conquerable to a point where it doesn't keep you from enjoying them. This is the difference between action and reaction. Some people are so afraid, that they are unable to enjoy a roller coaster. The very thought of riding one can trigger an anxiety attack for some! This can result in some sort of paralysis of thought or action and occasionally a flight response. The same can be said of fighting or pre-fight fear, it can be paralyzing. To overcome this we must train physically, mentally and spiritually, training ourselves to withstand greater and greater amounts of conflict and chaos. The most successful way to do this for the martial artist is to train in a curriculum where the spiritual/moral and the mental/reflexive training meets or exceeds the physical. In so doing, our actions (be they reflexive or otherwise) are motivated by purity of action or clarity and not by a fear based reaction that is outside of our control.

Section 4: Spiritual and Moral Training

This, the third and final level of training, relates to all other levels of training. Spiritual and Moral training is directly related to volition or will. You must have the will to succeed or win. You cannot be passive and expect victory. It won't happen. I see this repeatedly in the martial arts; a student trains for years in techniques but is crushed by a street bully. This doesn't happen because of technique refinement on the aggressors part, rather it is almost entirely a matter of will or spirit and perhaps instinct. A good street fighter does not care if he will be hurt or he accepts it as a part of the deal. In many cases, a fighter won't even know they have been hurt until long after the encounter. Some of this is psychological, some of this is volition, and some of this is physiological. The martial artist falls into a trap when day after day they train in the touch antics of many martial arts schools. This type of training says you can fight without being hurt. It is a false assumption, which leads to disillusionment and fear. It can lead to the abandonment of training on one hand or the martial artist who is ever seeking the "magic pill" that will keep them safe. Sorry. It just doesn't exist.

On a personal, spiritual, level it is possible to look at every trial and every success as training for future hurdles and trials. It is my belief that we will continue to suffer and fail at the most basic of trials until we begin to view them as a method of training. Once we begin to be trained by our mistakes in judgment, actions or decisions we will no longer encounter those same mistakes and we will experience personal physical, mental and spiritual growth.

Section 5: Final Thoughts on the Categories

The three categorizations of training are each unique in that one part may be trained with little obvious effect on the remaining two parts. This however, is to do the whole of training and life in general a disservice. All three categories make up man, and for the greatest benefit, all three need development. One cannot develop just the mind. For that is to think about walking and never walk. You cannot develop walking without thinking about it. For that is to walk blindly into traffic. You cannot walk and think without contemplating what the step means. For surely you will not get where you need to go.

Section 6: Other Issues in Training

Within these six different categories there is also the need to train individually as well as with a partner. Each has a place. Individual training is necessary for the refinement of movement and probably more than anything, about the process of thought, that training individually generates. You must THINK about what you are doing. On the other hand, partnered training is also about refinement of movement but extends further into refinement of application through a process of sensory input. This is the primary difference between partnered and individual training. One utilizes the senses primarily while the other must utilize thought primarily. Both are necessary and when both can be combined in equal portions the greatest growth occurs.

Generally, growth or learning takes place in three basic forms: memorization, application, and exploration. Each of these can be utilized within the context of individual and partnered practice. However, the value of the individual and partnered practice will determine the speed at which a person will make it from memorization to exploration.

The issue is, "How can I practice in a way that makes my individual practice most valuable?" This is a question that plagues every martial artist or anyone whose chosen form of output requires interaction. The short answer for the pesilat is the inclusion of Rasa within their practice. Rasa is the heart or the will. Without it, your practice is empty and will not produce the results you hope for.

The most basic way to utilize Rasa within your practice is through the art of visualization – imagining an attacker, and responding with ferocity, confidence, and accuracy with both your mind and body in concert. This method has been used for generations because it works. Even imagining you can increase flexibility while stretching will help to increase your stretching capabilities over time. In many ways, you might consider visualization a type of hypnotism for the self.

Another way to utilize and develop Rasa also has similar properties to hypnotism and is through the art of focusing. Focus is something often spoken about in the martial arts, but is rarely explained. Essentially, focus is another term for the idea of concentration. Visualization is a type of focus but is more creative in nature, the basic element of learning to focus, might be to simply stare without blinking for as long as possible while someone attacks you. Additionally, you might develop focus by practicing to attack a very specific target on a training partner and not deviating from the attack until forced too by your opponent. These are outward expressions of focus that may also help you to develop greater focus. However, the development of focus can take place all throughout the day for most of us. For example, how about when a colleague three cubicles down is telling a joke and is being loud or disruptive? You have a choice to be distracted by them and join in or stay focused on your tasks and complete them. Once you are done you can enjoy the freedom of participating in that type of activity, knowing that your tasks are completed.

6b: Creating Value in Partner Training

This section is vitally important. I have already addressed a portion of it in the section on "Creating Value in Individual Training." The truth is, a good trainer is vitally important. It is impossible to develop a high level of ability without a good trainer or trainers. The purpose of this section is primarily to teach the qualities of a good trainer so that you will know what you need to do as a trainer and what you should expect from a trainer.

A training partner should be thought of as a trainer, similarly to how we might view the boxer whose trainer is encouraging them and making them work, pointing out areas to be improved as well as challenging them. Too often our trainers in the martial arts don't even punch at the target area. This is a bad situation that leaves both the trainer and the trainee deficient.

One way to be a good trainer was mentioned in the section on individual training – that is, that a trainer should be conscious of attacking a specific target. This not only trains the trainee but also the trainer gets to learn how to use Rasa in their attacks. This does not necessarily have anything to do with speed or power, but intention. If you intend to strike the stomach, aim for it! Don't aim off to the side of the stomach in anticipation of a parry or block that is coming. It cheats you as well as the trainee. Additionally, don't be afraid to ask someone to re-do an attack until you get a desired outcome. In other words, don't let your pride get in the way of your growth!

A good trainer is not abusive. So what if a trainer can give you a hard time when you are training something! It doesn't mean a thing. After all, it is the point of training to EVENTUALLY be good at what you are training, not immediately good at it.

A good trainer will push you to improve, testing your capabilities with mild resistance to your technique here and there until ultimately you are able to deal with it. The trainer should not necessarily try to defeat the technique (which in itself is unrealistic) but rather they should seek to improve your technique. All too often we get this wrong. It makes no difference if you can defeat a technique you know I am practicing, while I am practicing it. That really just shows your inability to be a trainer.

In PSP we try to develop counters to techniques that generally let the person complete the technique they started and put us in a position of advantage that has essentially adapted to their technique.

Chapter 17: Conclusion
Section 1: Final Thoughts

It is hoped that this book has given you a general sense of what PSP entails and that it will encourage you to study further. Be sure, there is more material to be discussed and even the material covered in this volume could be discussed much further. However, this manual was only meant to show the Tunas or "Bud" of the flower of Pencak Silat Pertempuran, much like the videos and DVD's.

Look for future volumes to include studies of the Jurus-jurus, Pembasmian, Latihan Berpasangan, Harimau, Senjata, Sambut Pukul and Beladiri, as well as the Kebatinan of Pencak Silat Pertempuran.

For more information on Pencak Silat Pertempuran or to arrange for seminars, training, etc. please contact Pencak Silat Pertempuran at info@combat-silat.net or visit our website at www.combat-silat.net

Chapter 18: Dictionary of Silat Terms

This Dictionary is meant to be useful for all students of silat and as such will include terms not necessarily in use in Perguruan Pencak Silat Pertempuran, however, those terms which are part of our Perguruan will be specially marked. Additionally, some of these terms have been collected over many years and from many different sources. Not all of the terms have been verified for accuracy so it is possible that the meanings may not be correct. As well, there are different dialects represented. Please send any corrections to info@combat-silat.net also; please understand that any errors are strictly a product of my own understanding of a term.

To use this dictionary, search for the word alphabetically. In addition, use the phonetic spelling to learn how to say the word. The structure of the phonetics shown is broken up by sounds. For instance, the phonetic "aah" is normally pronounced similar to the "a" in "water". The phonetic "ee" is pronounced like "ee" in "peer". The phonetic "ss" is pronounced like the "s" in sing. The single "t" is pronounced like the "t" in try. The phonetic "oo" is pronounced like the "oo" in look. The phonetic "i" is pronounced like the word "I".

Term	Meaning
Abang **PSP**	Elder sibling. **Pr.** aah-baahng
Adat **PSP**	To show respect. **Pr.** aah-daah-t
Akang **PSP**	Older brother. **Pr.** aah-kaahng
Ales **PSP**	Evasion from Pamur Silat. **Pr.** aah-less
Ales Badan **PSP**	Body Evasion. **Pr.** aah-less baah-daahn
Ales Kepala **PSP**	Head Evasion. **Pr.** aah-less ke-paah-laah
Aliran **PSP**	This is more about an association of styles. The association can be very loose. For instance, Pencak Silat Pertempuran is an Aliran Pamur. That is to say, that much of PSP was founded on ideas, concepts, practices, etc. that are found within Pamur. It is also possible to consider PSP an Aliran Sterlak since it also has much in common with Sterlak. **Pr.** aah-leer-aahn
Amerindo Silat	A combination of silat styles but mostly Mustika Kweetang silat and taught in the U.S. by Guru James Ingram.

Amir	State Director – literally leader. **Pr.** aah-meer
Anak Buah *PSP*	Member of the family. More specifically, anak=child buah=fruit. **Pr.** aah-nahk boo-uh
Anfal Dasar	Basic attacking punches, strikes, kicks, etc. **Pr.** aahn-faahl duh-sar
Angkat *PSP*	A type of throw where the leg is lifted typically. **Pr.** aahng-kaah-t
Apa Khabar / Apak Khabar *PSP*	Greeting: What's the news?
Arit	A sickle, another term for Clurit / Celurit often used in pairs or with another weapon.
Asideci Silat	A Silat system created by Guru David Jennings and accepted by IPSI as an authentic silat system. Primarily of Balinese descent.
Asli	Genuine, original, authentic
Ayam *PSP*	Chicken. **Pr.** i-yaam
Lawi Ayam *PSP*	Rooster Claw the name for the larger version of "kerambit". **Pr.** laah-wee i-yaam

Ba Pak / Bapak *PSP*	Bapak, Ba Pak, Pak - Father but also used to show respect for ones teacher. Usually shortened to Pak. For instance Pak Roedy, Pak Bruno, etc. **Pr.** baah-paahk
Badan *PSP*	Board; body; torso; group; agency; corporation
Bagimana? *PSP*	How are you?
Baik-baik sekali. Dan Anda?	Very fine. And you?
Baju Melayu	The Malaysian silat uniform.
Baju Silat *PSP*	Silat Uniform **Pr.** Baah joo
Bangau *PSP*	Crane
banting / bantingan	Throw, throw down forcefully
Baru	Innovator.
Beladiri *PSP*	Self-Defense. **Pr.** bell-aah-deer-ee
Belakang *PSP*	Back
Belati	A type of knife.
Belok *PSP*	Turn or Crank
Belok Kepala *PSP*	Head crank takedown.

Bengkung	Belt used to mark the level of one's study in silat.
Berbelah Bagi	Half-hearted
Berbohong	To tell a lie.
Bercakak	Part of Speech: Verb Meaning: to fight
Berhormat-hormatan / hormat-menghormati *PSP*	Show mutual respect; salute each other. **Pr**. bare-hor-maaht
Berhormatan	Shortened version of showing mutual respect. **Pr**. ber-hore-maaht-aahn
Berhormat Resmi	Formal bow.
Beri hormat	Extend regrets; salute.
Beri salam / selamat	Greet say hello, extend greetings; salute
Bersenam	Verb: To do physical exercises.
Beset / Biset	A block/check, which is performed by moving the leg backwards. Often thought of as a rear sweep but that is a misnomer.
Bintang *PSP*	Star
Biru	Blue
Bohong	A lie, falsehood.

Buah *PSP*	Fruit – In silat it is used to refer to applications or techniques found in the jurus.
Buang	Literally: Throw away! Sometimes used to reference throws in Silat. **Pr.** boo-aahng
Buka *PSP*	Opening
Bung *PSP*	Fellow, buddy; elder brother (affectionate title for some popular leaders)
Bunga / Bungo *PSP*	Bunga, Bungo - Flower – In silat it is used to refer to the artistic movements of the style and sometimes as fake Buah to mislead and opponent. **pr.** boong-gaah
Bunga Kembang	The second level of bunga in PSP. **Pr.** Kem-baahng **Lit.** flowering
Bunga Mekar	**Pr.** mee-kar **m.** flower
Bunga Tunas	**Pr.** Too-naahs **m.** flower bud
Cabang *PSP*	Branch – In silat it is usually used in reference to a branch location of a given style and also as a weapon similar to the Japanese Sai with larger and wider spaced tines. Can also be used as a reference to certain Tankgapan. **Pr.** tjaah-baahng

Cakak / Cekak *PSP*	Fight; fighting. **Pr.** tjaah-kaahk
Campur Anduk	All mixed up.
Campuran *PSP*	Blended or mixed. Used in reference to silat systems that contain components of various styles of silat. I.e., Mande Muda, Pertempuran, Gerakan Suci, and most other silat systems depending on how far back you trace them. **Pr.** tjaahmp-er-aahn
Carok *PSP*	Random fight. Often associated with the Madurese. **Pr.** tjaah-roke
Celing Taring / Celeng Taring	Boars Tooth Strike. A strike where the thumb is used to press or hit into specific points on the body. **Pr.** Tjel-eng taah-ring
Celurit / Clurit *PSP*	Similar to a scythe or grass hook. **Pr.** tjaah-loor-it
Cepat *PSP*	Fast. **Pr.** tje-paaht
Cikalong	A style of Silat from Java
Cikgu	Malaysian for teacher
Cimande / Tjimandie	A style of Silat from Java.
Cinkrik	A style of Silat from Java
Dalam *PSP*	Inside, Inner. **Pr.** daah-laahm
Dampal	Sole of foot.

Dampal Tangan	Palm of hand.
Dapuan *PSP*	Front sweeping kick. **Pr.** daah-poo-aahn
Datuk Maha Raja Diraja	King of Kings
Debawa	Low. Sometimes-just bawa. **Pr.** deh-baah-waah
Delapan *PSP*	Eight. **Pr.** del-aah-paahn
Dengan Hormat	With respectful greetings.
Depan *PSP*	Front, in collocation with 'di'. **Pr.** deh-paahn
Depok *PSP*	When the rear leg steps in front of the front leg in a cross stance or the front leg steps backward in front of the rear leg. **Pr.** deh-paahk
Diri *PSP*	Self; stand; exist. **Pr.** deer-ee
Dorong *PSP*	Push, Impel; urge into being interested; motivate. In many Sumatran styles it is the name given to the straight punch. **Pr.** doh-rohng
Dua *PSP*	Two. **Pr.** doo-aah
Dua Belas *PSP*	Twelve. **Pr.** doo-aah bel-aahs

Duduk *PSP*	Sitting with legs crossed "indian style". Sometimes used for kneeling as well. Different from Sila. **Pr.** duh-dook
Empat *PSP*	Four. **Pr.** Em-paaht
Enam *PSP*	Six. **Pr.** En-aahm
Gajah Putih	White Elephant Silat known for its excellent use of elbows at close range. From Java.
Garak Garik *PSP*	Strategy that basically means for every action there is an appropriate counter. **Pr.** gaah-raahk gaah-rihk
Garuda	Bird. Sometimes used to describe an eagle
Gegaman	Hand weapon
Gelek *PSP*	Turning into a cross stance. Weight either equal or mostly on the front leg. Could be used for evasion but not necessarily. **Pr.** geh-lehk
Genggam *PSP*	To grasp in the fist.
Gerak *PSP*	To Move. See: Gerakan
Gerak Dasar *PSP*	Basic Movements

Gerakan **PSP**	Specific Movement. In Raja Sterlak these movements are used during the training of Bunga and stalking an opponent as well as in PSP. **Pr.** Ger-aahk-aahn
Gerakan Dua **PSP**	A reference to the second Gerak. The Vertical Movement of Raja Sterlak Silat
Gerakan Empat **PSP**	A reference to the fourth Gerak. Inside Circle of Raja Sterlak Silat
Gerakan Lima **PSP**	A reference to the fifth Gerak. The Four Corners Slapping of Raja Sterlak Silat
Gerakan Satu **PSP**	A reference to the first Gerak. Horizontal Gunting Movement of Raja Sterlak Silat
Gerakan Tiga **PSP**	A reference to the third Gerak. Outside Circle of Raja Sterlak Silat
Golok **PSP**	A type of machete. **Pr.** go-lohk
Gunting **PSP**	Scissors. **Pr.** goon-ting
Gunting Kaki	Scissors Kick.
Gunung	Mountain
Guru **PSP**	Teacher of many things. Can include spiritual training as well as fighting. **Pr.** Goo-roo

Guru Baharu	Beginning guru. Similar to guru muda.
Guru Bruno Cruicchi	Garrote Larense and Raja Sterlak teacher from Caracas Venezuela
Guru Jim Ingram	Teacher of Amerindo Silat
Guru Muda *PSP*	New/Young Teacher
Guru Muda Bayu Wicaksono	New Teacher of Pamur Silat. See Pamur
Guru Roedy Wiranatakusumah	Teacher of Jati Wisessa Silat
Guru Silek / Guru Silat *PSP*	Teacher of Silat
Guru Tristan Sutrisno	Teacher of Pencak Silat Cimande
Guru Tua	A "ripe" or old guru. Someone who has been around the block so-to-speak.
Halang	To block. **Pr.** Haah-laahng
Hantaman	Blow, smack, punch.
Harimau *PSP*	Generally used to describe ground fighting in silat. Also a style of Silat that specializes in ground fighting to include: prone, sitting, kneeling and standing. **Pr.** Har-ee-mow

Harimau Duduk *PSP*	Sitting Tiger. A kneeling posture of Pamur Silat and Pertempuran Silat. **Pr.** Har-ee-mow duh-doohk
Hati-hati	Be Careful!
Hijo	Green
Hitam	Black
Hormat *PSP*	Culturally acceptable behavior as defined by the culture itself. **Pr.** hor-maaht
Hormat Saya *PSP*	Greeting: My Respects
Hulubalang	Commander, war chief; district chief (in Aceh)
Huruf	Alphabet. In context of silat it means all those things that form the beginning stages of skills. **Pr.** hoo-roof
Ibu *PSP*	Wife. **Pr.** ee-boo
Ikat *PSP*	A bandana worn in various ways depending on the area of Indonesia a person is from. Javanese generally where it with the pointed part of the bandana covering the neck and the knot tied on the forehead. Sumatrans generally where it with the point of the bandana covering the head.

Ikat Badan	Large piece of fabric that is worn around the waist. **Pr.** Ee-kaaht Baah-daahn
Ikat Kepala *PSP*	Basically a large bandana. Color, size, and method of wearing, can be codified by the perguruan silat but not necessarily. **Pr.** Ee-kaaht Keh-paah-laah
Ilmu	Magic. **Pr.** Il-moo
Ini Keluarga Saya	This is my family
IPSI	Nomenclature for the Indonesian Governing body of International Pencak Silat. Most U.S. practitioners and teachers do not belong to it.
Jagabaya *PSP*	Village constable in Java. Regional director in Silat Pertempuran. **Pr.** jaah-guh-by-aah
Jagoan *PSP*	A person who fights. **Pr.** jaah-go-aahn
Jari *PSP*	Finger. **Pr.** jar-ee
Jari Dua Tunjal	Two Finger Poke. **Pr.** jar-ee doo-aah toon-jaahl

Jari Lubang	To make a hole in something with your finger. More of a picture of what the outcome could be than an actual hole. Used to reference single finger strikes. **Pr**. jar-ee loo-baahng
Jari Pecut	Finger Whip. **Pr**. jar-ee pet-joot
Jari Tombak	Spear Fingers. **Pr**. jar-ee tome-baahk
Jari Tunjal *PSP*	Finger Poke. **Pr**. jar-ee toon-jaahl
Jari Tusuk *PSP*	Finger Stab. **Pr**. jar-ee too-sook
Jati Wisesa Silat	Full name is Seni Bela Diri Silat Jati Wisesa. A style of silat that is almost identical to Gajah Putih. The only difference is the inclusion of Panafersan. **Pr**. Jaah-tee Wih-say-saah see-laaht
Jatuh *PSP*	Falling. Pr.
Jurus / djoeroes / djurus	Upper body patterns of movement mainly, although they can contain kicks and stepping methods as well.
Jurus-jurus	Plural of jurus, which typically refers to upper body movements. **Pr**. djoo-roos-djoo-roos

Jurus Bintang *PSP*	The 5 angles of attack: straight, from right side, from left side, downward and upward. Pencak Silat Serak uses a 9-angle system, as does Hok Kuntao, although the angle numbers are different. **Pr.** djoo-roos bin-taahng
Jurus Celurit *PSP*	Jurus that define the use and movements of the Celurit. See Celurit.
Jurus Duduk	Jurus that are done while sitting. Purpose it to isolate upper body defense. Usually used in beginning stages of training.
Jurus Gajah Putih	Jurus of Gajah Putih Silat.
Jurus Harimau *PSP*	Jurus of Harimau Silat or relating to Harimau movements within another style.
Jurus Kerambit *PSP*	Jurus that define the use and movements of the Kerambit. See Kerambit.
Jurus Kombinasi *PSP*	Combinations of Jurus-jurus much like a kata or kuen.
Jurus Pamur *PSP*	Jurus of Pamur Silat.
Jurus Pisau *PSP*	Jurus that define the use and movements of the Pisau. See Pisau.

Jurus Raja Sterlak	Jurus of Raja Sterlak Silat.
Jurus Tangan *PSP*	Jurus that are specific to empty hands.
Jurus Tongkat *PSP*	Jurus that define the use and movements of the Tongkat. See Tongkat.
Jurusan / djoeroesan	Two man set of attacks and counters based on the movements found in the jurus-jurus.
Jurus-jurus *PSP*	Correct way to say more than one jurus. Bahasa typically doubles up the word it wishes to pluralize.
Kabau / kerbau	Water buffalo - Relates to silat through the origin story of the Minangkabau people of Sumatra.
Kakak	Brother and sister.
Kaki *PSP*	Leg/foot. **Pr.** Kaah-kee
Kaki Ayam	Chicken Foot. Can be used to mean barefoot.
Kaki Lengket *PSP*	Sticky Legs. A type of Langkah training for leg trapping. **Pr.** Kaah-kee leng-ket
Kalajaking / Kalajengking / Kampret / Kalang *PSP*	Scorpion. Also Kala, and kalong. **Pr.** Kaah-laah-jaah-king

Kanan *PSP*	Right. **Pr.** Kaah-naahn
Kapala / Kepala *PSP*	Head (body part), be in charge of. **Pr.** Keh-paah-laah
Kasih salam	Greetings with affection.
Kawan	Friend - but not real close. **Pr.** Kaah-waahn
Kawan Seperjuangan	Comrade-in-arms.
Kebatinan / Kebatinin *PSP*	Spiritual Study. Inner Self. In silat it is usually a reference to spiritual training sometimes including the use of Ilmu. **Pr.** Keh-baaht-in-in
Kelapa *PSP*	Coconut. **Pr.** Keh-laah-paah
Keluarga *PSP*	Family. **Pr.** Keh-loo-ar-gaah
Kembali	You're Welcome. **Pr.** Kem-baah-lee
Kembang *PSP*	Flowering. The meaning within PSP is the act of development. Similar to Intermediate. **Pr.** Kem-baahng
Kendang *PSP*	Musical Drum. **Pr.** Ken-daahng
Kendang Penca *PSP*	Music specifically for silat created mostly with kendang. **Pr.** Ken-daahng Pen-tjaah
Kendang Tarompet	Music specifically for silat created mostly with Tarompet. **Pr.** Ken-daahng Tar-ohm-pet

Kerambit / Korambit / Karambit / Krambit **PSP**	A small hand sickle originally intended for use as a tool to harvest rice and later converted into a weapon. Of Sumatran origin. **Pr.** Kaah-raahm-bit
Keris	See kris. **Pr.** Ker-iss
Ketua	Chairman; elder, chief; moderator. **Pr.** Keh-too-aah
Khalifah	Literally it means commander. In Silat Gayong, khalifah is a pronounced instructor. There are many levels of khalifah- each with different level of responsibilty and authority.
Khatam	Completion of study. You may Khatam Silat meaning, "complete your studies of silat." **Pr.** Khaa-taahm
Kilat	Lightening. **Pr.** Kee-laaht
Kinjit Siku **PSP**	Body-throw usually using the elbow. **Pr.** Kin-jit see-koo
Kiri **PSP**	Left. **Pr.** Keer-ee
Kirim Salam	Send greetings or regards.
Komandan	Commander; commandant.

Kris	The blade of some keris is wavy, while others are straight. Usually the handle is removable for cleaning which is performed once a year in a citrus and arsenic bath. Traditionally considered to have spiritual powers. Sometimes spelled Keris.
Kucing	Cat. **Pr.** Koo-tjing
Kuda-Kuda / Kudo-Kudo *PSP*	Horse stance. Common stance in the martial arts with feet spread at least shoulder width and knees bent at least partially. Often used to deal with an opponent to either side. **Pr.** Koo-duh koo-duh
Kuda-Kuda Bangau	Crane stance. Standing on one leg with arms held similar to the wings of a crane. **Pr.** koo-duh koo-duh baahng-gow
Kuda-Kuda Belakang / Kuda-Kuda Kucing *PSP*	Back weighted stance or cat stance. **Pr.** koo-duh koo-duh Belaah-kaahng **Pr.** koo-duh koo-duh Koo-tjing
Kuda-Kuda Berat *PSP*	Strong stance. Usually a very wide base. Found in Pamur - Madura
Kuda-Kuda Kalong *PSP*	Sometimes referred to as S-stance. In Combat Silat it is the Bat "Stance". **Pr.** koo-duh koo-duh kaah-long

Kuda-Kuda Menengah *PSP*	Medium height Kuda-Kuda training. Mostly for defense. Good balance between mobility and stability. **Pr.** koo-duh koo-duh meh-nen-gaah
Kuda-Kuda Monyet *PSP*	Monkey Stance. Refers to the position when you squat equally with both legs, feet flat on the floor. **Pr.** koo-duh koo-duh mone-yet
Kuda-Kuda Naga	The Dragon Stance, when you squat down on one leg with the other leg extended to the side or front. **Pr.** koo-duh koo-duh Naah-gaah
Kuda-Kuda Rendah *PSP*	Low Kuda-Kuda training. Used mostly for ground fighting. Greater stability but less mobility. **Pr.** koo-duh koo-duh Ren-daah
Kuda-Kuda Ringan *PSP*	Narrow horse stance or high horse stance. **Pr.** koo-duh koo-duh Ring-aahn
Kuda-Kuda Tinggi *PSP*	High Kuda-Kuda training. Mostly for offense. Used when greater mobility is needed but not greater stability. **Pr.** koo-duh koo-duh Ting-gee
Kuda-Kuda Samping *PSP*	Side leaning horse stance. **Pr.** koo-duh koo-duh Saahm-ping

Kuda-Kuda Sedang *PSP*	Medium horse stance. A little wider, but not real wide! **Pr.** koo-duh koo-duh se-daahng
Kuda-Kuda Ular	Snake Stance. This is a ground position where one leg is fully extended and the other is bent, similar to the "hurdlers stretch". **Pr.** koo-duh koo-duh oo-lahr
Kujang	A type of knife with Islamic background. Contains a hook, serations, and typically an angled handle. **Pr.** Koo-jaahng
Kuku	Claw, Hoof, Fingernail. **Pr.** Koo-koo
Kuku Macan *PSP*	Earlier variant of the Kerambit. Translates to Tigers Claw. **Pr.** Koo-koo maah-tjaahn
Kumango	A style of silat from Sumatra.
Kunci / Kuncian *PSP*	To lock/a lock. **Pr.** Koon-tji-aahn
Kunci Mati *PSP*	Dead lock. Putting a pesilat into a position where they are unable to continue. **Pr.** Koon-tji maah-tee
Kuning	Yellow. **Pr.** Koo-ning
Langkah / Langka *PSP*	Step, steps or stepping. **Pr.** Laahng-kaah

Langkah Bintang *PSP*	A two-man drill where one person lies on the ground and the other uses various stepping methods to maneuver around the persons outspread limbs delivering knees, punches and elbows. **Pr.** Laahng-kaah bin-taahng
Langkah Dua *PSP*	The second step of Pencak Silat Pertempuran. Essentially performing a U shaped step or a side to side stepping method.
Langkah Empat Berpasangan *PSP*	Two man Langka Empat drill where opponents move in mirror like fashion around the Langka Empat Dalam. Can also be used to train hands, forearms, and Bunga. **Pr.** ber-paahs-aahng-gaahn
Langkah Empat Dalam *PSP*	Stepping method that is defined by the four corners of a square. Devised as an individual training method for the various stepping methods found in Raja Sterlak.
Langkah Empat Kembar	Name for the double square of Langka Empat. **Pr.** kem-bar

Langkah Empat Luar PSP	Stepping method that is defined by the four corners of a square but with four steps to each side of the square. Each corner uses Gelek/Depok to turn. Also to enter to the Langka Empat Dalam do so from the corner in an aggressive, larger step.
Langkah Garis PSP	Straight stepping. Could be called Langkah Satu. Also can be broken up into Langkah Garis Luar and Langkah Garis Dalam.
Langkah Jalan	Stepping method for walking on a straight line
Langkah Silang / Langkah Lima / Langkah Salib PSP	Stepping method for learning how to turn in all four directions using a cross pattern. **Pr.** Se-laahng **Pr.** Lee-maah **Pr.** saah-leeb
Langkah Tiga PSP	Used in some styles. This stepping method represents the use of the three corners of a triangle. **Pr.** Tee-gaah
Latihan PSP	Any of the many drills that are used for training. Actually, the whole of silat is latihan. **Pr.** Laah-tee-haahn

Latihan Berpasangan *PSP*	The way that Pencak Silat Pertempuran denotes drills that cannot be practiced without a partner. Usually they are not "curriculum" per se, but augment or develop attributes that are useful for understanding the curriculum or combat.
Latihan Berpasangan Bertenun Kaki *PSP*	Weaving Legs Drill. Similar to Kaki Lengket or Sticky Legs drill but basically stationary.
Latihan Berpasangan Bertenun Siku *PSP*	Weaving Elbows Drill. Similar to Hubad Lubad or Hubud Lubud of Filippino kali.
Latihan Berpasangan Bertenun Tangan *PSP*	Weaving Hands Drill. Similar to Hubad Lubad or Hubud Lubud of Filippino kali.
Latihan Berpasangan Pukulan Terus	Two man punching drill. 2 count with destruction.
Latihan Berpasangan Siku-siku Ular *PSP*	Elbow drill that requires to people to perform. Based on the constriction of a python for use in controlling the limb of an attacker.
Lawan	Adversary, attacker, enemy, foe

Lawi Ayam *PSP*	Rooster Claw the name for the larger version of "kerambit". **Pr.** Law-weeh ae-yam
Lempar	Toss, throw
Lengket	Sticky. Kaki Lengket is Sticky legs, Tangan Lengket is Sticky Hands. **Pr.** Leng-ket
Lima *PSP*	Five. **Pr.** Lee-maah
Lintau	A style of silat from Sumatra
Lompat Agos	To jump around or backwards.
Luar *PSP*	Outside. **Pr.** Loo-ahr
Luku	(Noun) plow. Can be used to describe an action that resembles plowing or clearing. **Pr.** Loo-koo
Lutut *PSP*	Knee. **Pr.** Luh-tooht
Lutut Celeng	Boars knee blow. Pr. Luh-tooht tje-leng
Ma Ha Guru Abdul Muthalief	Guru Cruicchi's teacher of Raja Sterlak and Selembam.
Maaf / Ma'af *PSP*	Forgiveness. **Pr.** maah-'-aahf
Macan *PSP*	Also Tiger. **Pr.** Maaht-jaahn
Macan Buntut *PSP*	Literally "tigers' tail." **Pr.** Maaht-jaahn boon-toot

Macan Tutul *PSP*	Panther. **Pr.** Maaht-jaahn too-tool
Maenpo	The application of Pencak Silat techniques.
Maganda	Beautiful.
Maha Guru / Ma Ha Guru	Master Teacher.
MaHa Guru Victor deThouars	Professor of Serak Silat.
Mahaguru	See Maha Guru.
Main Pisau Kuku Alang	Play of the eagles knife claw.
Main Silek	To play silek or silat. Equivalent to light sparring where the goal is to learn but not hurt your opponent
Main Terus Menerus	Continuous silat play. More similar to sparring
Mande Muda Silat	A prominent family form of silat in the US, which means "New Cimande". The late Pendekar Herman Suwanda was system head. Died in car crash September 2000. Oldest sister (Ibu Rita) is now the head of the Cabang.
Mandi Minyak	The oil-bathing test. You cook coconut juice until it produces oil and use the boiling oil as body lotion.

Mandi Seni	The ceremony a student must undergo before learning the art of weaponry in Silat Gayong.
Mas *PSP*	Friend. **Pr.** m-aah-s
Masukan *PSP*	Similar to Langkah but used to teach bridging or entries in Pamur Silat. **Pr.** maah-soo-kaahn
Masukan Kaki *PSP*	Term used to differentiate between leg entries and Masukan Tangan (hand entries) in Combat Silat.
Masukan Lutut *PSP*	Entry done with the knee.
Masukan Sepak *PSP*	Entry done with a kick. Not just a kick though, you must enter, either by pressing down the leg or stepping into a Masukan Kaki.
Masukan Siku *PSP*	Entry done with the Elbow.
Masukan Tangan *PSP*	Hand entries of Combat Silat.
Mati *PSP*	Dead. Used to describe the end of a technique or lock in silat. **Pr.** Maah-tee
Mekar *PSP*	Rising dough or blossoming flower
Melangkah	The consideration of how to step

Melayu / Malay	Anthropoligists: Sub-polynesians who dwell in the Malay Archipelago since the Stone Age and their descendants.
	Malaysian Constitution: Anyone who is Muslim, speaks the Malay language and practises the Malay culture.
Melutjuti / Melucuti Senjata *PSP*	Weapons disarming
Membohong	To tell a lie.
Mencekik *PSP*	Strangle, Choke.
Mencegah	To deter. **Pr.** men-tjaah-gaah
Menaruh Hormat	Give respect
Menjebak	To trap. **Pr.** men-jeh-bahk
Merah	Red
Menengah	Medium.
Menukar	To exchange **Pr.** men-yoo-kahr
Minangkabau *PSP*	The most prominent people group of West Sumatra who are known for the low fighting styles. Raja Sterlak is related to one of the 10 major styles of the area
Monyet *PSP*	Monkey. **Pr.** Mohn-yet
Murid *PSP*	Student. **Pr.** myuhr-id

Murid Mati *PSP*	Dead student - A method of training where the training partner does not resist. One part of the statue drill. **Pr.** myuhr-id maah-tee
Naga *PSP*	Dragon. **Pr.** naah-gaah
Napas *PSP*	Breath. **Pr.** naah-paahs
Olah Raga *PSP*	Competition fighting.
Olahjiwa Olahtubuh Olahhidup - Alam taka	Train the mind, train the body, develop your life, nature is your teacher.
Opsir	Military officer.
Pamur Silat	A Madurese silat style.
Pangianan Langka Empat Silat	A Sumatran silat style.
Panglima	High-class warrior, equivalent to the ranks of Arthurian knights. They serve sultans and often command the army to battles.
Papisau *PSP*	Knife hand strike. **Pr.** Paah-pee-sow
Pauh	A style of silat from Sumatra
Pecah *PSP*	To break. **Pr.** Peh-tjaah

Pecahan *PSP*	Usually means a breaking of something. Can mean to break apart a jurus or even a technique for a closer examination of individual components. **Pr.** Peh-tjaah-haan
Pecakak	Part of Speech: Noun Meaning: a person who likes to fight.
Peci / Songkok *PSP*	The name for the velvet hat that is worn by silat practitioners.
Pecut *PSP*	Flick. Whip. **Pr.** Peh-tjoot
Pelan	Slow.
Pelatih *PSP*	Trainer, instructor; (training) coach. Nothing beyond physical instruction is provided. **Pr.** peh-laah-tee
Pelatih Muda *PSP*	Group Leader in PSP. **Pr.** peh-laah-tee moo-duh
Pembasmian *PSP*	A series of methods in Pamur Silat that are designed to eradicate the opponent. Only used as a last resort. **Pr.** pem-baahs-mee-aahn
Pembohong	Liar
Pemukulan	Stick or staff used in pencak silat. Also referred to as Tongkat.

Pencak Silat / **pentjak silat** *PSP*	Generic term for silat systems of Malaysia, Borneo, Indonesia and the Philippines.
Pencak Silat Batak	Silat system taught by Guru Yusef Siregar that combines various Sumatran silat systems together. Guru Yusef is Batak so I have given the silat he taught my guru, the name Silat Batak.
Pencak Silat Manyang	The Manyang style originates from the Princely Madurese Family of Setiyo out of the village of Sumberpucung. By Raden Pandji Setiyo, Raden Pandji Setiyo Cipto, Raden Pandji Setiyo Suprapto and Ibu Raden (= princess) Aju Cetiyo Wati.

Pencak Silat Pertempuran *PSP*	Silat system which combines elements from Pencak Silat Pamur, Pencak Silat Raja Sterlak, Seni Bela Diri Silat Jati Wisesa, Pencak Silat Raja Monyet, Pukulan Pencak Silat Sera, Hok Kuntao and various Filipino stick fighting methods. Officially given the name of Pencak Silat Pertempuran in August of 2000 to symbolize the acceptance of this system by my Guru-guru Silat.
Pencak Silat Ratu Adil	A Dutch Indonesian System of Silat founded by Ma Ha Guru Rudy Terlinden.
Pencegah	Something that prevents or deters. **Pr.** pen-tjaah-gaah
Pencegah Tangan *PSP*	To check something with the hands. **Pr.** pen-tjaah-gaah taahng-aahn
Pendekar	A hero or great master of silat.
Pendiri Silat *PSP*	Founder of a silat system. i.e., "Pendiri Silat Cimande'. **Pr.** pen-deer-ee

Pengajar *PSP*	Teacher, instructor. Different from Guru, which offers spiritual guidance. Not a pendekar, which is more akin to a national hero or a Grand Master but does offer something more than physical instruction only. **Pr.** pen-gaah-jar
Pengajar Muda *PSP*	Beginning Instructor.
Penjebak *PSP*	To Trap like an animal. **Pr.** pen-jeh-baahk
Penjebekan *PSP*	Animal Trap. **Pr.** pen-jeh-bahk-ahn
Pentjak / Pencak *PSP*	The "artistic" side of silat. Beauty. See also Seni. **Pr.** Pen-tjaahk
Perguruan *PSP*	Being under the tutelage of a guru. A club of people. An organization. This can be new style of silat, which was founded by a particular master. **Pr.** Per-goo-roo-aahn
Perhatian *PSP*	Attention.
Perisai	Shield. **Pr.** peer-ih-sie
Permainan *PSP*	Short form of "main" is usually used. Means to play. In the context of silat it means to play silat. Usually a type of slow fighting and counter fighting. **Pr.** per-maah-in-aahn

Pernapasan / Pernafasan *PSP*	Breathing methods. Most styles of silat have breathing exercises for strengthening and some for the development of tenaga dalam or internal strength. **Pr.** per-naahp-aahs-aahn
Persatuan	Governing Body. **Pr.** per-saah-too-aahn
Persaudaraan / Persaudaran *PSP*	Brotherhood. **Pr.** per-sow-der-aahn
Pertukaran *PSP*	To exchange or change hands. **Pr.** per-took-aah-raahn
Pesilat / persilat *PSP*	Person who practices silat. **Pr.** peh-see-laaht
Picak *PSP*	Step on. **Pr.** Pee-jaahk
Picak Baru *PSP*	Light step. Seeing with your feet in essence.
Pisau *PSP*	Any type of straight blade Knife
Pitinggua	"Crane Stance" with the raised foot in front of the supporting leg
Prajurit *PSP*	Advisor **Pr.** praah-jewr-it **Lit.** Warrior, Soldier, Brave Soldier, Private.
Pukul / poekoel *PSP*	To beat or hit.

Pukulan / poekoelan *PSP*	Usually used in reference to street fighting systems of silat and kuntao. However, it can mean a specific punch. **Pr.** Poo-koo-laahn
Pukulan Belakang *PSP*	Backfist
Pukulan Gampar *PSP*	Slap Punch
Pukulan Gampar Membalik *PSP*	Inverted Slap Punch **Pr.** mem-baah-lik
Pukulan Kalajaking *PSP*	Scorpion Punch
Pukulan Macan Tutul *PSP*	Panther Fist. **Pr.** Poo-koo-laahn Maah-tjaahn too-tool
Pukulan Monyet *PSP*	Monkey Punch
Pukulan Naik *PSP*	Uppercut Punch **Pr.** Naah-ik
Pukulan Pamur *PSP*	A punch similar to the horizontal punch of most other martial arts, however, the chamber is at the shoulder versus the hip. Unique to Pamur.
Pukulan Sabit *PSP*	Hook Punch **Pr.** Saah-bit
Pukulan Sterlak *PSP*	A vertical punch that starts palm down and rotates. Unique to Sterlak Silat.

Pukulan Tedung	Cobra Fist. **Pr.** Poo-koo-laahn
Pukulan Terus *PSP*	Straight Punch **Pr.** ter-oos
Pukulan Tukul *PSP*	Hammer Fist **Pr.** too-kool
Pukulan Ular Sendok *PSP*	Cobra Fist Punch **Pr.** Oo-lar sen-dok
Pusaka / Pusako	An heirloom or something of value. Usually old.
Pusat *PSP*	Navel; center; center, central, main, Headquarters
Putar Kepala / Puter Kepala *PSP*	Head turning throw.
Putih *PSP*	White
Rahasia / Rahsia *PSP*	Secret
Raja *PSP*	A King. **Pr.** Raah-jaah
Rasa *PSP*	Feeling, emotion. **Pr.** Raah-saah
Rasa hormat	Respect
Rencong	A type of knife used by the Aceh people of Sumatra, which is sometimes held between the toes.
Rendah	Low. **Pr.** Ren-daah
Sabung	A fight between animals
Sabung Bebas	Free fighting. Similar to sparring.

Sabung Berpasangan	Fighting techniques
Sahabat *PSP*	Friend
Sahabat Karib	A close intimate friend
Sahabat Lama	An old friend, a long-time friend
Sahabat-sahabat	Friends
Sakalipan Gaja Menlintang, Gaja Raba! *PSP*	Sterlak motto meaning, "An elephant gets in my way, I knock it down."
Salam *PSP*	Peace (in greetings); greetings. **Pr**. saah-laahm
Salam Hangat	Warm regards.
Salam Hormat *PSP*	Greeting: Hello with respect
Salam Kompak	Warm greetings.
Salam Kompak / mesra	Cordial greetings, warm greetings
Salam Pembuka	Salutation
Salam Penutup	Complimentary close in letter
Salib *PSP*	Crucific. **Pr**. Saah-leeb
Sama-sama / sama sama	Exactly the same. Sometimes said same-same.
Sambut *PSP*	Similar to Buah. Basic applications of the jurus-jurus. **Pr**. Saahm-buuht

Sambut Pukul *PSP*	Applications of jurus-jurus but limited to those elements, which involve a striking element. **Pr.** Saahm-buuht Poo-kool
Sapik Kalo Silat / **Sapik Kala Silat**	A type of silat based off of the principle of striking whatever is closest. Not meant to mimic scorpion movements.
Sapu / Sapuan *PSP*	To sweep/rear sweep. A sweeping kick backward. Can be performed low but can also be done while standing. **Pr.** saah-poo-aahn
Sarong *PSP*	A piece of fabric, usually batik cloth, that is worn around the waist or around the shoulder. It can be one tube shaped piece of fabric that is woven or a single piece of flat cloth. Can be used as a weapon but more commonly used as part of the Indonesian dress for both male and female. Related to Islamic prayer times and the need to be covered to the ankles during prayers. **Pr.** Saah-rohng
Sarung *PSP*	Sheath of a knife. **Pr.** Saah-ruhng
Sasaran *PSP*	Training area. **Pr.** Saahs-aahr-aahn

Satu *PSP*	One. **Pr.** Saah-too
Saudara *PSP*	Brother **Pr.** Sow-dahr-aah
Saudari *PSP*	Sister **Pr.** Sow-dahr-ee
Sebelas *PSP*	Eleven. **Pr.** se-bel-aahs
Sekali Lagi *PSP*	Do it again. **Pr.** se-kaahl-ee Laah-gee
Selamat *PSP*	General greeting. Actually means safe. **Pr.** se-laahm-aaht
Selamat Datang *PSP*	Greeting: Welcome. **Pr.** se-laahm-aaht daah-taahng
Selamat hari lahir	Happy birthday.
Selamat Jalan	Greeting: Goodbye.
Selamat makan	Enjoy your meal.
Selamat Malam *PSP*	Greeting: Goodnight. **Pr.** se-laahm-aaht Maah-laahm
Selamat Pagi *PSP*	Greeting: Good morning. **Pr.** se-laahm-aaht paah-gee
Selamat siang	Good day (around noontime)
Selamat tidur	Good night, sleep well
Selamat tinggal	Goodbye used when one is being left behind.
Sembilan *PSP*	Nine. **Pr.** sembee-laahn
Sempai Hati *PSP*	Having the heart to do something.

Sempok *PSP*	A crossing step where the lead leg steps behind the rear leg, often into a sila position or the rear leg steps behind the lead leg. **Pr.** sem-paahk
Senam	Noun: gymnastics
Senaman *PSP*	Exercises, gymnastic like. Includes all forms of exercise to include rolling, etc. **Pr.** sen-aah-maahn
Seni *PSP*	Art or skill. Usually used in reference to the beauty of pencak silat movement. **Pr.** sen-ee
Senjata *PSP*	Weapons. **Pr.** sen-jaah-taah
Senjata Rahasia	Secret weapon.
Sepak *PSP*	To slap. To kick. **Pr.** Seh-paahk
Sepak Ayam *PSP*	Chicken Kick. Gets the name from the motion a chicken makes when scratching the ground.
Sepak Belakang *PSP*	Back Kick. Sometimes referred to as Tendangan Belakang when the heel is focused.
Sepak Bulat *PSP*	Roundhouse kick using the toe or ball of foot primarily.
Sepak Bundar Lompat	Jumping Crescent Kick

Sepak Cakeng / Bulat *PSP*	Roundhouse kick. With shoes use the toe to strike specific points. Related to Totokan.
Sepak Depan *PSP*	Front Kick. Sometimes referred to as Tendangan Depan when the heel is focused.
Sepak Depan Berpasangan *PSP*	Two man drill for front kick where one kicks and the other slaps the kick down then immediately kicks.
Sepak Iris *PSP*	Cutting Kick. Low sepak Rusuk using the edge of foot.
Sepak Gunting / Gunting Kaki *PSP*	Scissors Kick.
Sepak Kadam	Kick with sole of foot
Sepok Menyendok *PSP*	Scooping Kick. Used primarily to kick the groin in a scooping action.
Sepak Naga *PSP*	Dragon Kick. Usually more of a press than a kick, but not exclusively.
Sepak Rusuk *PSP*	Side Kick. Usually done to the ribs or torso. Can be Tendangan Rusuk when heel is focused.
Sepak Sekop *PSP*	Shovel kick.
Sepak Tundik *PSP*	Intercepting kick.
Sepuluh *PSP*	Ten. **Pr.** Se-poo-loo

Sera Silat	Owl. Relates to wisdom. Also the name of a Silat system.
Serdadu	Mercenary, soldier.
Sewar *PSP*	Sumatran knife that is narrow and has about a 10-inch blade with a slight curve and a handle that fits in the palm of your hand. Similar to Tumbuk Lada. Main difference is in the protuberance of the sarung. The Sewar has a straight protuberance while the Tumbuk Lada is usually bulbuous and representing a flower. **Pr.** see-waah
Sihir	Black magic. This forbidden practice can grant someone supernatural powers but always at an uncompromising price. The rituals are dark and ungodly, sort of worshipping Satan. Silat Gayong is free from any form of sihir.
Sikap *PSP*	Demeanor; attitude. **Pr.** See-kuhp
Sikap kuda-kuda	Stance.
Sikap Pasang *PSP*	Welcoming Postures of Silat Pertempuran **Pr.** See-kuhp paah-saahng

Siku / Sikut *PSP*	Elbow. Also represents the horizontal elbow strike of PSP. Can be done both tinggi and rendah. **Pr.** see-koo
Siku Belakang *PSP*	Rear elbow strike.
Siku Dalam *PSP*	Inner elbow strike.
Siku Datar	Horizontal elbow strike.
Siku Depan *PSP*	Front, rising elbow of Seni Bela Diri Jati Wisesa Silat.
Siku Diagonal *PSP*	Diagonal elbow strike.
Siku Jatuh *PSP*	Falling Elbow. **Pr.** see-koo jaah-too
Siku Membalik *PSP*	Overturned elbow. **Pr.** See-koo mem-baah-lik
Siku Naik *PSP*	Rising Elbow. Also known as Kapong. **Pr.** see-koo naah-ik
Siku Perisai	Elbow shield.
Siku Siku	A weapon similar to the Japanese Sai with larger and wider spaced tines. **Pr.** see-koo see-koo
Silah / Siloh *PSP*	Sitting cross-legged. **Pr.** See-laah
Silahkan tolong	Please help.
Silat Batin	Batin in silat deals with metaphysical phenomenon.

Silat Macan	Another tiger style of silat from Java. Mostly upright.
Silat Monyet *PSP*	Monkey style silat. AKA Pamonyet
Silat Olaharaga	It is the sports kumite of silat. More or less like the kind of sparring you would see in kickboxing or karate championship with, of course, its own rules. Grippling and leg sweeping are allowed. International events that hosts silat olaharaga are the SEA Games and the World Silat Championship.
Silat Panglipur	A traditional West Javanese Silat system.
Silat Pulut	This is a performing art normally practised during wedding ceremony. It is merely a graceful dance with stances and movements akin to silat-the-fighting-thing. Not for street fighting.
Silat Serak	The name of a Javanese Silat style prominent in the U.S. and brought by Dutch-Indonesians.

Silat Syahbandar	A style of silat that uses a shuffling motion but contains no langka per-say. Moves close to opponent by shuffling feet but without taking a "step".
Silat Tapak Suci	A style of silat
Silat Tjimindie	See Tjimindie.
Silat Tjinkrik	Old spelling for Silat Cinkrik. A system from Java.
Silek / Silat *PSP*	Fighting. Often used by itself to describe certain indigenous styles of martial arts from Malaysia, Indonesia, Borneo, Phillipines, Cambodia, Thailand, Laos, etc. The addition of the term Pencak is recent. Only within the last 50 years or so was that term used by IPSI
Silek Baru	A style of silat from Sumatra
Silek Tuo	A style of silat from Sumatra
Sitaralak / Stralak / Terlak / Tiralak / Tralak	Different ways of saying Sterlak
Slaverse *PSP*	Term Guru Cruicchi uses to describe the Jurus Kombinasi of Raja Sterlak.

Sterlak *PSP*	No known meaning even by the Indonesians. Could have been derived from the Dutch Staart Lag meaning "to render below".
Suliwa *PSP*	To pass or redirect
Sumatra	Island of origin for Sterlak Silat, Harimau, Kumango, Lintau, Puah, Tuo and Baru silat.
Sumbalik	Counter
Sumpah	Oath, solemn promise
Sumpit *PSP*	To shoot with a blow-gun
Sumpitan *PSP*	Blow-gun
Sundot	A jab or quick thrust
Suntok	Punch
Syahbandar	Harbour-master. Also name for a system of Silat
Tanaga Dalam / Tenaga Dalam	Inner Force. Can be thought of a person's will but other mystical ideas are also attached to this term. Similar in idea to Chi or Ki
Tanda hormat	Sign of respect; salute
Tangan *PSP*	Arm/hand

Tangan Lengket *PSP*	Sticky Hands. A type of training which teaches the student how to control their arms as well as those of the attackers. Develops hand-trapping skills.
Tangkap / Tangkapan *PSP*	To catch/a catch. Used in reference to grabbing a punch. In Sundanese it is called Daywak. Also, The locking techniques of Silat Pamur. **Pr.** Taahng-kaahp-aahn
Tangkis *PSP*	Interception block to stop opponents' hitting power by jamming. **Pr.** Taahng-kiss
Tapak *PSP*	Palm. In Silat Seni Gayong Tapak refers various locks, etc. **Pr.** Taah-paahk
Tapak Belakang	Back palm strike.
Tapak Gampar	Palm slap.
Tapak Tumit	Palm heel strike. **Pr.** Taah-paahk too-mit
Tari / Tarian / Pentari / Pentarian	Dance / a dance / a dancer / dancing

Tari Piring	Plate Ballet. A form of dance associated with silat training where a plate is held in the palm of ones hand and various movements are performed without dropping the plate. Minangkabau silat.
Tari Sewah / Sewar	Dance with the Sewah / Sewar. Dance with the knife.
Tarik Kepala *PSP*	Literally Head Pulling Throw. This is done without the turning of the head associated with Putar Kepala.
Tarompet	Musical Horn
Tataran	Rank, level
Tedung	Cobra
Tenaga Dalam	Internal energy, similar to KI or CHI.
Tendangan *PSP*	Heel Kick. **Pr.** Ten-daahng-aahn
Tendangan Belakang *PSP*	Rear heel kick. **Pr.** Ten-daahng-aahn bel-aah-kaahng
Tendangan Depan *PSP*	Front heel kick. **Pr.** Ten-daahng-aahn de-paahn
Tendangan Rusuk *PSP*	Side heel kick. **Pr.** Ten-daahng-aahn ruh-soohk
Tendangan Ular Sanca *PSP*	Python kick. A derivative kick from Sepak Naga. **Pr.** Ten-daahng-aahn oo-lar saahn-tjaah

Tentara	Army
Tepisan	Parry to the side. Tangkis can be a parry also but sometimes referred to as a block.
Terima Kasih *PSP*	Thank you. **Pr.** Teer-ee-maah kaahs-ee
Terima Kasih Banyak	Much Thanks!
Tiga *PSP*	Three. **Pr.** Tee-gaah
Timbilan *PSP*	Term used for the throws and takedowns of Pamur Silat. **Pr.** Tim-bee-laahn
Timbilan Kaki *PSP*	Takedowns mostly involving the use of the legs. Can include sweeps, trips, pressing or kneeling. **Pr.** Tim-bee-laahn kaah-kee
Timbilan Tangan *PSP*	Takedowns mostly involving the use of the hands. Pushes, press, pulls, etc. **Pr.** Tim-bee-laahn taahng-aahn
Tinggi *PSP*	High. **Pr.** Ting-gee
Tingkat *PSP*	Level. **Pr.** Ting-kaaht
Tjimindie / Ciminde	A kuntao/silat system brought to the U.S. by Guru Willie Wetzel.
Tongkat *PSP*	A pole or staff. **Pr.** Toeng-kaaht

Totokan *PSP*	Point striking, nerve attacks. **Pr.** Toe-toe-kaahn
Tuah	Magic power, Good Luck, Good Fortune
Tujuh *PSP*	Seven
Tulen	Original
Tulup *PSP*	Blow Dart Gun
Tumbuk Lada	Sumatran knife that is narrow has about a 10-inch blade with a slight curve and a handle that fits in the palm of your hand. Similar to Sewar. Main difference is in the protuberance of the sarung. The Sewar has a straight protuberance while the Tumbuk Lada is usually bulbous.
Tunas *PSP*	Bud of a flower. Represents the beginning of something. **Pr.** Too-naahs
Ucapan selamat	Congratulations
Ular *PSP*	Snake. **Pr.** Oo-lahr
Ular Sanca *PSP*	Python. **Pr.** Oo-lahr saahn-tjaah
Ular Sendok *PSP*	Another name for Cobra. **Pr.** Oo-lahr sen-dohk

| Ustaz | Title for religious teachers. Some pesilat call their instructors as Ustaz. |

About the Author

Sean Stark, a practitioner of a variety of martial arts, was first introduced to pencak silat by Guro Dan Molash during his time training in Hok Kuntao. After this introduction he knew that pencak silat was the martial art that would hold his interest and fuel his passion. Already a martial artist with a varied background; including Hok Kuntao, Kali, Arnis, Animal Kuntao, Combat Kempo, Garrote Larense and various other arts. Guru Stark decided to pursue something deeper by devoting himself to the development of pencak silat and its culture within the U.S.

Today, Guru Stark holds seminars and provides training around the country and internationally to help people get a first hand glimpse of pencak silat whenever possible.

Guru Stark holds a BFA, in graphic design from the University of Wisconsin and currently works for a mission organization in the areas of print and web design, as well as digital photography. In addition, he continues to teach Pencak Silat to those who are interested and operates a successful website devoted to the dissemination of information concerning pencak silat. www.combat-silat.net

10177975R00211

Printed in Germany
by Amazon Distribution
GmbH, Leipzig